WELSH
CHAPELS

WELSH CHAPELS

ANTHONY JONES

SUTTON PUBLISHING

AMGUEDDFEYDD AC ORIELAU CENEDLAETHOL CYMRU
NATIONAL MUSEUMS & GALLERIES OF WALES

First published in 1984 by National Museum of Wales

Fully revised and expanded edition first published in 1996 by
Sutton Publishing Limited
Phoenix Mill · Far Thrupp · Stroud · Gloucestershire
in association with
National Museums & Galleries of Wales

Reprinted 1996

British Library Cataloguing-in-Publication Data

A catalogue record for this book is available from the British Library.

ISBN 0-7509-1162-X

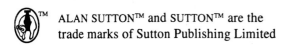
ALAN SUTTON™ and SUTTON™ are the
trade marks of Sutton Publishing Limited

Typeset in 11/12 Times.
Typesetting and origination by
Sutton Publishing Limited.
Printed in Great Britain by
Ebenezer Baylis, Worcester.

Contents

Acknowledgements

All illustrations are by the author with the exception of the following: Y Lolfa, 16; National Library of Wales, 39, 50; Pontypridd Library, 107; National Museums & Galleries of Wales, Museum of Welsh Life, 10; and the official chapel histories, reproduced with thanks.

My thanks to the Director of the National Museums & Galleries of Wales, Colin Ford, for his kind invitation to revise and republish the original text for the booklet *Welsh Chapels* which I wrote for the Museum in 1984 as an accompaniment to the exhibition of my photographs of the chapels. That work, and this, was the result of inestimable help from the Board of Celtic Studies of the University of Wales, and the Research Foundation of Texas Christian University, Fort Worth, which I gratefully acknowledge. My appreciation also to Jaqueline Mitchell of Alan Sutton Publishing for her patience and tolerance of my tardiness, and Richard Levy at the Royal College of Art, London, for his darkroom magic. I would especially like to thank Hywel Davies of Nant Films, and HTV Wales, for the opportunity to present two television documentaries in 1995 on the history and the current plight of the chapels. I am not alone in being so fond of the chapels of Wales, nor in trying to help to preserve their remarkable history, and I must express my appreciation and thanks to John Hilling, Alan Vernon Jones, John Harvey, Vernon Hughes, Warne John, Graham Rosser, Professor Ieuan Gwynedd Jones, the National Museums & Galleries of Wales (Museum of Welsh Life), and the membership of CAPEL, the non-denominational group who are doing outstanding work in documentation, for everything they have done and continue to do for the chapel heritage.

During the years of fieldwork and research in Wales I was always met with courtesy and enthusiasm by people who are in some way associated with chapels, so my thanks to the many deacons, ministers, chapel secretaries and treasurers, the many 'keepers of the chapel key', and others far too numerous to mention, all of whom made a contribution to this attempt to gain a general overview of a vast and complex subject.

Finally, these words and pictures about the chapel heritage are dedicated to the memory of my fathers, Edward Jones and Emrys Rees; to my family in Anglesey, Mountain Ash and Merthyr Tydfil; to my patient and wonderful wife, Patty Carroll; and to my son, Edward Emrys Jones, in Texas.

Introduction

I confess I am not an objective critic. Childhood impressions are indelible; I am forced to feel that more and more. . . . You have not seen the old chapel at Llanuwchllyn, by the still water, the roof no higher than that of the villagers' houses around it. Its walls were bare, except where patches of damp had given a slight variation to the colour; the benches were sometimes comfortable and sometimes hard – according to the sermon; the windows long and narrow and without ornament, save when the frost drew pictures on them. And yet, that is the most beautiful place where I have ever been. It is the place where I began to think, it was where I fell in love for the first time, there I felt the dread of damnation and the joy of forgiveness; my ambition was first aroused there, and my pride laid low by having it enforced upon me that I was wholly without merit – every thought and feeling of greater profundity than the course of daily living, human and divine, direct me back to that old grey chapel. It was void of all architectural and pictorial beauty, but through a window opposite our bench I could see the rain driven by gusts of wind across the mountain-slopes, and a rowan tree curved by the prevailing winds into a form of such elegance that it would be the despair of any artist to reproduce the delicate beauty of its branches. The old chapel and its people are greatly changed, now, but when thoughts of heaven visit my unsettled mind – you will probably smile to hear me say so – but paradise to me is like the old chapel at Llanuwchllyn – the people seated in families on the benches, everyone just the age they were, the preaching, the jubilant singing, the plaintive sigh of the wind, and that old rowan tree. . . .

Sir Owen M. Edwards, *O'r Bala i Geneva, from* A Book of Wales, *ed. D.M. Lloyd, Collins, 1965*

The streets and byways of Wales are nowadays littered with the decomposing hulks of chapels, hundreds of abandoned Bethels and Bethesdas. These were the Nonconformists' temples, the 'Palaces of the Oral Arts' that once trembled at the passionate preaching of an inspired minister, and shook to the resonance of massed congregational hymn-singing. The chapels of Wales were once the architectural celebrities of every street and country lane, but now they crumble quietly and await the ministrations of the bulldozers that will turn these landmarks into wasteland.

As a child in Wales I was once told, with breathtaking brevity, that there were only three religions in our world, 'The Roman Church, the English Church, and the Nonconformist Church, which is owned by the Welsh'. The non-Anglican Nonconformist church denominations grew out of the seventeenth century in Wales, and by the early years of the twentieth century Nonconformity was 'owned by the Welsh', and had overwhelmingly established itself as the national religious expression. The buildings erected by the Nonconformists, their modest chapels, simultaneously became the national architectural expression of Wales.

This book is about those chapels, so is therefore an attempt to grapple with but one part of a vast subject: the dramatic conversion of the slumbering agricultural Wales of the seventeenth century into the dynamic industrial powerhouse it became in the nineteenth and early twentieth centuries. In part it describes the intimate relationship between that extraordinary transition and the Nonconformists, and their chapel buildings – they built thousands of them, large and small, charming and pompous – for the Nonconformists were such an essential force in every aspect of Welsh life that they literally affected the entire culture of the nation. It concentrates on the chapel buildings, because they are the physical repository of that history, but an architectural heritage that is under increasingly active and hostile threat.

In an effort to convey the flavour of the meaning of 'chapel' in its wider sense I have sought to place the buildings at centre-stage, but while they are the most dominant characters in the drama of modern Welsh history, they stand before a complex back-drop of shifting scenery, and cannot be seen in isolation from it. I have tried to describe that back-drop as the scenes changed over the two hundred years in which the chapel played such a central role. They often directly affected that drama, while at other times the force of action upstaged the chapels, and they were more reactive than proactive. Where possible I have quoted comments from the characters of the period, and let their voices speak from the dusty scripts of the old chapel histories (with an anticipation that their ghosts will forgive the lack of individual attributions).

The word 'chapel' means much more than simply a building reserved for worship purposes on Sundays. For anyone familiar with Wales, and especially for those who were born or brought up there, the word triggers in the mind a flood of associations that range from the unforgettably terrifying sermons of those preacher 'kings of the pulpit' to Sunday School Bible class, the huge tea-parties, the annual bus excursion to a temptation-less and inhospitable beach, the singing festivals, baptism ceremonies, the Band of Hope meetings, marches and processions . . . associations that remind us that the chapel was at the heart of every community in Wales until the mid-twentieth century, it was the essence of so much of the culture, politics, sociology, education, religion, economics, and shaped the psychology of the nation.

Religion has been judged today – especially by the young – as mostly irrelevant, and without a young congregation to inherit the faith and traditions and carry them onward, the chapels will fade away. Nonconformity, once the beating heart of life in Wales, is rapidly disappearing as a force of any significance, so the chapels that were its home are going too. They have long been viewed as not worth saving, and rather insignificant as architecture. The result has been that they are being closed, abandoned, vandalized and demolished at an ever-accelerating pace. Yet these fascinating and often beautiful buildings, mostly overlooked, tell an extraordinary story, that of the transition of Wales from a seventeenth-century agricultural society of unsaved people, to a hot-bed of industrial revolution, social upheaval and change, into a God-fearing nation where, in the nineteenth century, three-quarters of the entire population was attending chapel of a Sunday. The history of that transformation is contained in the stone-and-slate chapels of Wales, for they stand as the physical symbols of a driven evangelical mission and a faith that captured the hearts and minds of the Welsh, who made Nonconformity the national religion. The chapels that they built were in Wales, of Wales, and for Wales: those buildings were in those centuries, without question, the national architecture of Wales.

The chapels of Wales come in all shapes and sizes, and the very 'different-ness' of each of them is part of their fascination. Some are exceedingly modest structures, others are pompous and grand, some plain and others elaborately ornate. While there are many that are beautifully-proportioned and finely-crafted, there are also many brutal boxes. The forces that conspired to build them also guaranteed – as we shall see – that they were all different, but perhaps there is one thing that for many years they all had in common, and that was that they were dismissed as having 'no architectural merit'. They have been variously described as 'blots on the landscape', 'horrible heirlooms', 'insensitive amateur exercises', 'brash little conventicles'.

Some have said that Welsh chapels may be buildings but they are not architecture, dismissed the Nonconformists' efforts in 'building brash conventicles', and mocked the early chapels as 'incomparable with Churches'. They missed the point. One cannot apply the same standards to the chapels of this period as one can to the churches; they may share a common worship-purpose, but there the similarity ends. Concentrating on chapels as parallel works of architecture applies to them a contemporary response, one those early Nonconformists would not have understood because the idea of consciously creating something that was considered as 'architecture' was completely irrelevant to them. Until the middle of the nineteenth century they had other priorities and objectives that did not stress such a grandiose concept as architecture. Indeed, it took the chapel-builders from 1689 (when they began to build) to 1872 to erect what was described as 'a cathedral of Nonconformity' (Tabernacl, Morriston). Instead, what they wanted was a simple building, sturdily built, with a modest appearance, which was to be plainly furnished in a domestic style that emphasized the seamlessness of the faith they held at home and the faith they publicly professed in chapel. Lack of irrelevant decoration in the creation of the Bethel, and of any hint of ostentation was paramount. Chapel-building was the antithesis of church architecture, and the last thing the Nonconformists wanted was to be compared to the Anglican Church in this way; what they wanted was a chapel that was as humble and unpretentious as they were themselves, a place that was – to use the much-loved Welsh phrase – 'serviceable and tidy'.

A notorious defamation of Wales and the Welsh was published anonymously in 1910 under the title *The Perfidious Welshman*, and its author noted of chapels:

> The hideous creations called 'chapels' – especially the pepper-pot style favoured by the Calvinistic Methodists – are nothing more than the social clubs of the countryside, whither the black-coated faithful resort, not to pray forgiveness for their real or imaginary sins, but to air their politics and pass resolutions for the damnation of the English Church. . . . The chapels are an insult to the Almighty, a stain upon the venerable soil on which they stand, the quintessence of ugliness unadorned, they kill all natural beauty that may surround them . . . they 'dissent' from every known canon of art and beauty.

> *Anonymous, writing under the name 'Draig Glas', in* The Perfidious Welshman,
> *Stanley Paul, 1910*

The Welshman's Reputation (by 'An Englishman') was the heated reply to a book full of such slander, though it failed to find much to say in defence of chapels:

> The Welshman has been said to evince an incapacity for building, a distaste for architecture, and a lack of aesthetic perception in the style of his chapels. It may be so. We are indebted to Wales for some of the best of our slates in grey and purple, but it must be said that old Silurian stone is not the easiest to work into a form . . . granite, limestone and sandstone do, however, occur in Wales, and the best buildings will naturally be found where the most suitable material is to hand . . . and if the castles of Wales are attractive, the chapels are admittedly ugly . . . and who is responsible for the 'pepper-pot' chapel and its 'pigeon-loft' style of decoration – why, the Welsh builder, of course. . . . Yet it was a Welshman who wrote 'The Grammar of Ornament'! But the chapels are there in Wales, in their 'bizarrerie', and what is bizarre is positively ugly, not simply plain.

> *Anonymous, writing under the name 'An Englishman', in* The Welshman's Reputation,
> *Stanley Paul, 1910*

As recently as 1995 Sir Wyn Roberts, Minister of State in the Welsh Office, in evidence to The Welsh Affairs Committee, stated: 'We are constrained by the need to preserve outstanding buildings, architecturally . . . historically many of the chapels, as I recall, were in fact built to a standard pattern and they are not particularly distinguished buildings . . . there are not all that many of them in existence that are in fact worth preserving, or that call for preservation.'

The result of all this dismissive comment is a classic case of ignorance leading to accelerating neglect and decay, and the easily-perceived loss of a vital part of the material culture of Wales. It is curious that until the mid-1980s this heritage has not been something that the Welsh have generally noticed or been proud of, and very little effort has been made to halt the wholesale demolition of chapel buildings. The protection of Listed status afforded many other structures has been slow to be applied to chapels, and there has been little real care for the local, regional and national architectural expression they embody. The climate of opinion may, however, be changing, for some individuals and institutions, and a non-religious group of architectural enthusiasts called CAPEL, have been making an heroic effort to conserve the chapel heritage by recording the disappearing buildings, and helping to preserve documents and artefacts associated with the chapels.

A comprehensive study of the meaning and effect of the Nonconformity in Wales would be an enormous undertaking, for the impact it had on the formation of modern Wales from about 1700 to 1900 was immense and affected every aspect of life in the country. The Nonconformists and their chapels evolved from a position where they were reviled dissenters who left the Established Church and converted rude farm-sheds and barns into places of their kind of worship, to the single most important force of faith and influence in Wales, whose chapels were the focal point of every community. The chapels are an essential part of any study of Wales since 1700, for they represent an extraordinary achievement by a population that fell under the potent spell of a religious vision: ordinary people toiled to make their visions into temples. What they built became a compendium of the religious, social, political, economic and cultural history of Wales, and thus they are the physical repository of that history. Likewise, there is a vast corpus of material relating to the history of the chapels which is widely scattered across Wales in private hands, national collections and commissions, local libraries, records offices, museums, local history collections, denominational associations, and in the chapels themselves, but this has yet to be drawn together in any nationally coordinated way.

Nonconformity became the dominant force in every part of Wales, and for many the chapel often represented the only accessible spiritual and cultural focus available to the population. It had this central role because it was far more than being uniquely or 'only' a place of worship. It fulfilled a community role as a church, school, library, concert hall, art gallery, debating society, place of sisterhood, temperance society, and the locus of musical and choral expression. For all these reasons the word chapel means far more than simply the building that housed a worshipping congregation, and thus the far-reaching effect that a chapel had in communities cannot be overestimated.

I hope that from the following jumbled pageant of places, buildings, preachers, statistics, opinions (favourable and venomous), architects, historians, personalities, anecdotes, dry facts and curious tales the identity of what 'chapel' really means in Wales will be revealed.

. . . It may be argued that the most expressive architecture in Wales is that of the chapel. Its span touches at its nether ends tin shacks and fake baroque, but throughout the countryside there are hundreds (one had almost said thousands) of stone chapels, shapely, dignified, and apt for God's worship, which keep within a firm tradition and yet give opportunity for local and denominational variation. For long the heart of both community and national life, they are genuine folk-architecture. Today their power weakens, but for three Welshmen out of four the gleam of a varnished pew, the ecstatic rustle of a rising congregation, and maybe the taste of a hymn-book cover, are unforgettably part of those childhood days when, in sensuous innocence, we stood a rung nearer to Heaven.

Gwyn Jones, A Prospect of Wales, *Penguin, 1948*

CHAPTER 1

The Roots of Dissent

WELSH CHAPELS: WHAT AND WHY ARE THEY?

What were the forces at work that created a phenomenal change in society and culture in Wales? What had caused the Welsh to begin the huge chapel-building phenomenon that was such a vital characteristic of urban and rural Wales in the nineteenth century? What urges drove the congregations of every Nonconformist denomination to strive to build these thousands of chapels? What did the massive and sudden industrialization of Wales mean to Nonconformity, and what did the chapel-builders contribute to that revolution? Why were the chapels such a significant part of the visual, literary, musical and social culture of Welsh society? Who designed and built them? Why do they look as they do? Who paid for them? Why are they now in such a catastrophic state of decline and decay? What efforts are being made to preserve the chapel heritage? What have chapels meant to Wales? What exactly is a chapel?

A chapel is actually not a building, but a *congregation*, or (as they were sometimes called) 'a community of believers' who came to 'meetings' or 'gatherings' (rather than to 'worship services'). Thus these early Nonconformists were called 'gathered churches' (i.e. they met because they were 'gathered by the Spirit of God'), who came to a meeting-house, the place that would eventually become known as their chapel.

To begin to answer so many questions and place the chapels in a context, one must draw a rather direct line through a complex subject, by joining the Puritans of the seventeenth century to the later Dissenters and Conventiclers, and to the Nonconformists who built the chapels. In doing so, albeit simplistically, one realizes that as far as that history is concerned there is a readily-identified purpose for the chapel, and that purpose is ultimately the only reason the chapel exists: it is a house for a *pulpit* from which to hear *preaching*.

> . . . Thousands of our people know Christ as neither God nor Man, as priest and prophet, have never heard of Him! O, forlorn and desperate state. Preaching is in many parts unknown. Shall we be in ignorance until we all have learned English . . . can we not have preaching in our own tongue?
>
> *John Penry, 'A Plea to Parliament', (1580), in Thomas Rees,* History of Protestant Nonconformity in Wales, *John Snow, 1883*

1

The fundamental reason for Penry's 'Plea to Parliament' is linked to the core belief of the Nonconformists that preaching was of overwhelming importance. The pulpit therefore assumes a literal and metaphorical focal-point in both Nonconformist thought and in the chapel buildings themselves. The significance of preaching cannot be underestimated for it was the root cause of the aggravation between the Established Church (i.e. the Church of England or the Anglican Church), and those who dissented from it, and was the issue that in the seventeenth century would ultimately lead to the founding of the independent Nonconformist denominations we know today as the Congregationalists, Unitarians, Baptists, Methodists and Presbyterians. The story of that transition is a complex one, but for our purposes in asking why the Welsh chapels were built, and how Nonconformity flourished in Wales, we can conveniently focus on the unifying concern over *preaching* as the most significant single issue, joined with that of preaching and evangelizing in the *Welsh language*.

Although there are many variations of exterior styles and treatments, in every chapel, at its very heart, is the symbolic architectural focus of the congregation's faith: the *pulpit*. The Nonconformists share a fundamental common belief that the congregation has come together for essentially only one purpose, to worship by hearing *y Gair*, the Word of God, addressed to them from that pulpit. Thus it is the reason for the existence of the building: it is the kernel around which the chapel is merely an elaborate shell.

The history of the Puritan-Dissenting movement in Wales and its earliest chapel buildings, is a long and fascinating one, that cannot be told in detail here. Suffice it to say that in spite of horrendous persecution from 1662 to the Act of Toleration in 1689, Nonconformity was a hardy sapling that had put down deep roots, refused to be dislodged, and grew into 'the mighty oak of Welsh Dissent' in the nineteenth century. The single thread that runs through the history of Dissent is its followers' belief about the importance of preaching, and that belief was to result in the basic plan of the chapels that were to house them. The preachers sermonized in a direct and uncomplicated way in the vernacular of the day, and likewise the style of their chapels was to be rooted in the vernacular architecture of Wales when they came to be built.

The first true Dissenters' chapel was established at Llanfaches, Mon., in 1639, 'The Jerusalem of Wales', and laid emphasis on preaching in a direct and engaging manner to large congregations who were especially susceptible to vivid, poetic, passionate and imaginative preaching expressed with warmth and engaging sincerity. The result of the foundation of Llanfaches during the Commonwealth years was described in graphic terms: 'the Gospel ran across the mountains like a fire in the thatch'.

Attempts to reconcile the Dissenters with the Established Church failed, and Dissent became an underground movement, but one that was based on powerful faith and would not be persecuted out of existence. The core beliefs remained unchanged:

that the congregation had entered into a personal covenant with God that required no Church ritual or liturgy, and that their lives should be a combination of reticence, self-imposed austerity, and a desire to hear preaching, that would lead directly to the architectural expression of their chapel buildings.

At times of harshest persecution they returned to gatherings at night in inconspicuous dingles in the hills and woods, caves, and remote barns. There is no contemporary documentary account by those Nonconformists of quite what it was like to attend an illegal conventicle in the days of persecution, but the following passage captures the essence of the experience:

> Cwmglo was inconspicuous, a dingle of sylvan beauty, screened by a profusion of dense copses and tall overhanging trees. . . . But even in the delicious seclusion of Cwmglo the Dissenters were not free from molestation. Though their minds were fixed on the things of the spirit, their ears were always alert for the footsteps of the informer. A shaking bough, or a quivering bush, or the snap of a twig in the undergrowth, made their hearts beat faster, their blood run cold. The soothing influence of hymn and sacred song was denied them . . . hostile ears might be listening in the thickets. On wintry nights, not for them the cheery gleams of the modern street-lamp. The only light to guide their faltering footsteps was afforded by the moon or stars. When the sky was overcast they stumbled over trackless mountains in an inky darkness that only country people know. . . . Hidden in the trees around Cwmglo was a gabled farmhouse of considerable dimensions. . . . Its occupier was himself a Dissenter, and when his fellow worshippers requested of him the use of one of his barns for a chapel, we may be sure that he readily acquiesced. An empty barn all the year round on a farm well-known for its productive meadows might, it was thought, arouse the suspicions of an erstwhile passer-by. To delude the curious, therefore, the barn was stored with hay during the weekdays, and emptied for the services on Sundays. The congregation was not seated when the service was in progress – a standing position was more conducive to instant dispersal should escape become necessary. The rostrum was crudely built of timber felled in the contiguous woods. A rush light that flickered wanly in the draught from the ventilation holes in the walls, provided the only illumination . . . and to keep themselves warm they wrapped their feet in straw. . . .

> *Tom Lewis*, History of Hen dŷ Cwrdd, Cefn-coed-y-cymmer, *Gomer Press, 1947*

Each Nonconformist congregation that gathered as a church was completely independent of any other congregation, and recognized no central authority to define or rule on how it conducted itself: all decisions were made by the individual independent congregations. They were said to be 'not a denomination, not a sect, not even a society, but an attitude, a manner, a way – whatever word you choose', and the defining word that they did choose was *chapel*.

Each chapel zealously guarded its independence from all others, and quite what this tenacious independence meant when congregations began to build chapels will be seen in due course.

CHAPTER 2

The Late Seventeenth Century: 'Toleration' and the First Chapels

I n 1689 the Act of Toleration generally freed the Nonconformists and brought to an end the State-supported period of repression and persecution. Nonconformity was still subject to certain constraints, but the Act allowed for Dissenters to have licensed chapels and to build meeting-houses. Even though the law was to protect the Nonconformists, it still did not save them from unruly mobs intent on destroying their chapels:

> The Sabbath meeting for worship at the chapel, but great numbers of people gathered together in a riotous manner and exceeding disturbed that meeting with clamour and noise, and by throwing in a vast number of stones of several pound weight, to the defacing of the house, the breaking of the windows, and the terror of those within. When peacefully departing they were set upon in the street, abused, beaten, stoned and pursued through the streets of the town. The *cwnstabs* [the constabulary] were absent, being withdrawn to a small alehouse outside the town.

> *Thomas Rees*, History of Protestant Nonconformity in Wales, *John Snow, 1883*

In spite of such harassment the Nonconformists set about creating meeting-house chapels in which to gather for worship and preaching. Most of these chapels were conversions of existing buildings, mostly farm-barns and the like, but a few were newly built. There is virtually no documentary evidence of what these chapels looked like, but they were sound and serviceable, built according to the local traditions of scale and proportions, with simple but solid craftsmanship, of materials readily to hand. They were in almost every case to be speedily replaced by other structures as congregations grew when the great religious revivals washed over Wales. From the Act of Toleration in 1689 to 1715, some 38 known Nonconformist chapels were created in Wales. Only one from that period, Maesyronnen (1, Plates 1, 2), near Hay-on-Wye, still exists in anything like the original form. Among the conversions of barns and erections of new chapels in this period are the adaptations of an old Anglican church in 1690 at Llan-y-bri, and a town hall in Flintshire in 1701, while the congregation in Llanbryn-mair continued to meet from 1675 to 1739 in a farmhouse with a lean-to chapel from the conventicle days.

The reliable historic records show that there were 3 new chapels built in Monmouthshire, 7 in Glamorganshire, 9 in Carmarthenshire, 4 in Pembrokeshire, 4 in Cardiganshire, 3 in Breconshire, 2 in Radnorshire, and 6 sprinkled over North Wales. However, it is likely that there were others that escaped recording, and documentation of the period is very incomplete. The Nonconformists were not too forthcoming about themselves: they were great students of the Bible and recalled the injunctions against numbering the people of God.

The chapel buildings of the Nonconformists in Wales were the result of a mixture of tumultuous social, economic, political and religious forces acting together, and sometimes in conflict, to provoke in the nineteenth century a building frenzy – it was called 'chapel-mania' – that affected every denomination, and also spurred the Anglicans to build anew throughout Wales. That eventual mania, however, began with the building of the first very modest chapels.

Early Dissent had a strong character of itinerant preachers abroad throughout Wales, not bound to one place. Nevertheless, a natural urge to have the church gather in a meeting-house that was specific to its needs quickly established itself, and as a result the word chapel came to mean both the congregation *and* the building in which they worshipped. Once chapels 'as buildings' were established, congregations then tended to advance their evangelizing from these fixed points which became magnets, drawing people to them to hear inspiring preachers and become engaged in the social activities of the congregation. After years of hardship, persecution and concealment, the Nonconformists wanted to establish themselves publicly, and to build meeting-houses: 'What had been sown in tears, would now be reaped in joy, and the chapels are our sheaves.' But what were those chapels to be, and what should they look like?

The early chapels were built by congregations who simply did not care what the Established Church thought of people who worshipped in a converted cow-shed. They had been forced to meet in such places before so it seemed not to matter to them that they would continue to do so, provided that such places were now properly cleaned and prepared, and provided with what they called 'a worshipful atmosphere'. The congregations embarked on the fitting-up of buildings as meeting-houses, though they increasingly used the word chapel to describe their place of worship. The essence of the endeavour of these 'Enthusiasts' was to create a functional preaching-room, and their chapels are crisp simple designs, prim little meeting-houses that were as unassuming, dignified and austere as the faithful who erected them. It was a 'folk architecture' that had a very clear stylistic recollection of the domestic and agricultural buildings of rural Wales. It was a reference that they were happy with, for it implied that the building was at one with the land and their faith, and a natural expression of both.

1 The oldest surviving chapel in Wales, Maesyronnen, near Hay-on-Wye, was converted from a cow-house in 1696, and is still largely in original condition. Most chapels from the period of Maesyronnen and into the 1700s were similar conversions . . .

In remote countryside at Glasbury, Rad. (near Hay-on-Wye), on a beautiful elevated site with sweeping views over the mountains and the valley of the Wye, stands the only extant chapel from the early days of Toleration. The survival of Maesyronnen Independent chapel (1, Plates 1, 2) in a form and condition that is reasonably close to original is surprising as successive waves of religious revival were to lead to congregations outgrowing their old chapels which, combined with natural deterioration of old structures, usually led to major rebuilding, enlargement, changes to the interior, but mostly to demolition and rebuild, and the majority of congregations cannibalized the old buildings, reusing the materials in the new chapel. Thus chapel-building is essentially organic in character, the congregation growing, and the chapel growing and changing with it.

Maesyronnen, however, is largely unchanged, and gives a fascinating insight into the original form of these early Nonconformist buildings. It is the key to understanding all subsequent chapel buildings. It was registered as a chapel in

2 . . . but even new purpose-built chapels retained this vernacular architectural style and looked like barns or the traditional Welsh longhouses like Cilewent Farm, Rad., built around 1750.

1697, though a congregation had been meeting secretly there to worship in a barn or byre called *y Beudy*, described as a 'cow-house', since the 1640s. Although Maesyronnen is architecturally and historically grouped with the converted barn-chapels of the period, it may have been largely purpose built. Certainly, it was built on the site of the old cow-house, part of which may have been incorporated into the new chapel, with the most reliable evidence showing that Maesyronnen was raised in 1696–7.

The chapel has a rectangular plan some 55 ft by 26 ft, with a small house attached to the western gable wall. The cow-house was originally attached to a substantial Elizabethan-period house, long-demolished, and the cruck-truss between the chapel and the house reveals that this newer small house is on part of the site of the sixteenth-century house. The whole feeling and originality of appearance of Maesyronnen, sited at the end of a lane, is entirely consistent with farm-buildings (the direct relationship with domestic architecture is strikingly apparent if Maesyronnen is compared with a classic Welsh house-and-byre like Cilewent Farm,

Rad., of 1750 (2), now at the Museum of Welsh Life, St Fagans, Cardiff). The long-wall or side-wall facade has three tall mullioned windows, flanked by two entrance doors under gables and projecting eaves – though the sundial is an unusual chapel feature over the western door.

The small house attached to one end of the building is a *tŷ-capel* (chapel-house), built to accommodate the minister or custodian of the chapel. This integration of chapel-and-house is the earliest example of what was to become a standard design – the modest chapel and abode of the Nonconformist preacher, in contrast to the grander vicarage or rectory that the Churches built for their incumbents. This form remains a standard, especially in the rural areas, until well into the 1850s, and replays the layout seen at farms like Cilewent.

The design of Maesyronnen is seminal, and is very much that which will dominate chapel-building throughout the 1700s and well into the early 1800s, with little variation from this pattern. The ground-plan of these chapels is generally a long rectangle, though there are a few squared-plan variations. They have a variable height of elevation (depending on whether a gallery was being built inside), the construction being in random fieldstone chinked with mortar, sometimes covered with a cement plastering then whitewashed. The facades featured the entrance door or doors with windows between them. The significance of this was the relationship between these exterior elements and the disposition of the internal elements of the chapel.

In Maesyronnen's interior the dominant element is, of course, the pulpit which is placed in the centre of the long side wall opposite the facade, and immediately captures one's attention upon entering the building. The pulpit has a window behind it so that the preacher has light coming over his shoulder to illuminate the Bible, a dramatic arrangement that back-lit the preacher with a 'halo' of light. The roof is divided into six bays, and features strongly-defined lateral bracing, in an effort to stoutly clamp together the spreading walls.

The variation of this interior layout is the placing of the pulpit in the centre of the facade wall, again with the windows backlighting the preacher. This meeting-house style created an especially intimate atmosphere, with the preacher in his elevated commanding position being able to make eye-contact with every member of the congregation, who were arranged in a 180-degree sweep in front of him. This quality of directness and closeness so well articulated at Maesyronnen begins to evaporate in the nineteenth century when the gable-end facade 'auditorium' chapels come into their own. In these, worshippers are arranged less like a gathered congregation and more like a non-participatory audience.

Maesyronnen has retained much of its honest-to-God charm, and its interior (3, Plate 2) is especially important as it gives a clear example of the form and manner of Nonconformist worship practices, for all the components that were to become massively amplified in the vast Victorian temples are to be seen at this simple

3 The interior of Maesyronnen has the simplicity and quality of a well-scrubbed farmhouse kitchen, with a high pulpit against the long side wall, a deacon's table set before it, and a mixture of deep pews and benches – everyone had a good view of the preacher, for the pulpit and the sermon are the essence of chapel architecture in all its phases. Although chapels become much grander in the Victorian-Edwardian period, all the basic elements are here at Maesyronnen.

chapel. The pulpit is raised about two feet above the floor (originally it may well have been higher). From this position the preacher could see everyone, including those who were seated in the deep pen-pews, built with doors in an attempt to defy the bone-chilling combination of Welsh winters and very long sermons in an unheated chapel – the only fire here was the fire of their faith. The congregation wrapped their feet in straw to retain warmth and to combat the dampness of the beaten-earth floor – though this was replaced in the early nineteenth century with flagstones. The chapel is rightly proud of its place in the history of Nonconformity and has, unique in Wales, listed every minister since 1645 on the front of the pulpit.

Directly in front of the pulpit stands a large plank-table, flanked by two baluster-backed benches (dated 1728), and a fine six-legged table used for communion. The elders and senior membership sat at these tables, in front of and below the minister. This arrangement of 'protective pews' around the preacher may be a recollection of the kind of protection needed by itinerant field-preachers and evangelists who were often threatened (and assassinated) by the mobs: friends who were strong in body and in faith gathered around in a semi-circle to ensure his safety. In Maesyronnen the same disposition is shown. It became a standard for all chapels and is popularly known at the *sêt fawr* or 'Big Seat', an enclosure in which the deacons would sit, and which became increasingly elaborate in the Victorian period. At this chapel, however, the simplicity of faith and the very humble origins of Nonconformity are still evident.

Sir John Summerson dismissed Christopher Wren's chapels for Cambridge University as 'mere rectangular cells for small congregations', a casual slight that the congregation at Maesyronnen would have accepted as both an accurate description and a compliment.

THE ARCHITECTURE OF ENTHUSIASM

Just as the many-branched Welsh oaks are peculiar to the Principality, so are these buildings – the natural product of the country, the true growth of the soil, and showing as clearly as any written history the development of the life of the people . . . but sad to relate that most of these ancient structures are in the last stages of decay, and therefore in a few years time these valuable pages of national history and native building will be lost forever. It is earnestly to be hoped that greater interest may be taken in them before it is too late.

Harold Hughes and Herbert North, The Old Cottages of Snowdonia, *1908, reprinted by Snowdonia National Park Society, 1979*

A chapel building like Maesyronnen is a very simple structure, but that simplicity becomes eloquent in the hands of those who assembled the parts, and who wanted their chapels to look like the traditional and familiar long-house buildings of the Welsh countryside. The overall effect was described by John Betjeman as 'the architecture of Enthusiasm'. It is domestic rather than glorious. There is no attempt to make the chapel a tantalizing reflection of the glory of Heaven-to-come, as was implied in the atmosphere of a great church or cathedral. Instead, the chapel-builders did what they knew best and built a simple room that was homely and comforting; this is an architecture of intuition, improvisation and ordinariness, not of grandeur. (The Shakers, a devout religious American sect that crafted beautifully-proportioned simple designs, observed that they made their furniture in the belief 'that an Angel might come and sit on it'. The simplicity of the early Welsh chapels is in accord with that observation, in their honesty and simplicity and their warmth of spirit: the congregations believed that an angel would be perfectly at ease and at home in their chapels.)

If there was a religious atmosphere, it was created by the preacher and the congregation in their worship, and not because of elaborate or heavily-decorated surroundings. They were suspicious of art and decoration as 'a snare set by the Power of Evil', and although the chapels were later to become a home to the visual arts, the latter were viewed as 'applied arts': they were applied to the service of religion and were never to be 'art for art's sake'. These congregations were naturally comfortable with this style of building as for years they had been erecting farms, cottages, barns and byres, and their chapels were at one with those structures. Their chapels were small, for the Welsh scale of things was overall smaller and humbler than that of England. John Betjeman famously wrote of these buildings in 1952: 'In their simplest form . . . the meeting-houses have the quality of a well-scrubbed farmhouse kitchen – a stone or tiled floor, scrubbed open seats, white walls and clear glass windows.'

The term 'vernacular architecture' deserves some interpretation as it serves in this context to link domestic building traditions with the chapels. Vernacular usually directly refers not to architecture but to building, the defining difference often being the involvement of an architect. A writer on the development of Welsh housing forms observed:

> Vernacular architecture is concerned not with great works of architecture designed by a professional architect at great expense and using the latest materials and technology, but with the homes of ordinary people built in the fashion traditional to that particular locality, using local materials with a minimum of expense and skill necessary. . . . New architectural ideas usually start with the upper classes and as their ideas pass down to those below, so the buildings of less wealthy people become increasingly architect-influenced. A large farmhouse of the sixteenth century would have been vernacular in style, but by the middle of the eighteenth century or the early nineteenth century, it would certainly have been built in a Georgian-inspired textbook fashion, and would have lost most of its local characteristics.

Eurwyn Wiliam, Home-made Homes, *National Museum of Wales, 1988*

That transformation in domestic architecture in Wales exactly parallels the development of chapel architecture from its grass-roots traditions to the often-meretricious architecture of the nineteenth century that disregarded the historic character of Nonconformity or Welsh building traditions entirely.

Wales in the late 1600s and to the mid-1700s was an essentially agricultural economy, and although Dissent and Nonconformity were centred on the southern border counties, and driven by a more advantaged class of the minor gentry, there was nevertheless very little, if any, disposable income to be lavished on the building of a chapel. John Betjeman once observed that 'What determines the architecture of a country is the people who pay for it.' These Nonconformists had as yet little money, and they had little knowledge of architecture, and not much interest in it either: it simply was not relevant in the context of building a meeting-house. In spite of the trend towards having a chapel many congregations could not consider building one, or had to make do with very spartan accommodation.

In rural Wales it took much longer for a congregation to assemble the funds to convert or build anew, and the tradition of meetings for prayer and discussion in farms and cottages continued. These were the traditional 'chapels as people' rather than as buildings. Tiny theological collectives were common in the countryside, but those around Bala were especially notable, in an area where woollens manufacturing provided essential income as a cottage industry separate from agriculture. The 'knitting-nights' at Bala were an informal and homely gathering, a domestic chapel for a community of believers who would knit socks in the large farm kitchens while discussing religious topics. Their work was easily portable and they travelled from farm to farm as a movable chapel. Their meetings involved discussion of a Scriptural subject, with a closing reading from the Bible and prayer. Through contributions and subscriptions and the sale of woollens, they gathered enough to build a chapel – though it took a mountain of socks to build a Bethel.

Congregations solicited friendly landowners to acquire donated land, but if they could not buy they would negotiate the lease for 999 years – the congregations believed that by then the Millennium would have dawned and the world would be owned by the people of God. The congregations contributed what they could to the building of their chapels, and instances of pawning heirloom watches and property to give the proceeds to the chapel fund are quite common, along with the selling of a lamb or a calf. When a generous donation was received they sometimes blazoned a thanks in the form of a plaque on the facade of the chapel, as at Three Cocks, near Brecon, in 1788: 'To the memory of £240, the pious donation of Thos. Williams, Gent., of The Island, Brecon, to and for the use and benefit of this chapel forever', while the community at large in Carmarthenshire in 1823 was thanked for a chapel 'Re-built by the contributions of this church of Christ here assembled, and the benevolence of the neighbourhood of Gwynfe'.

These early chapels demonstrate a very conscious desire to avoid any implication that a chapel was a 'church' in the sense of the Anglican Church, or any suggestion that the chapels of the Nonconformists were 'holy shrines'. As chapels became grander and more elaborate and expensive in the nineteenth century, many sharp critics of 'mad facade-ism' recalled the reticence and humility of these early congregations, and decried the 'Shriners' for abusing the memory of these early believers (to absolutely no avail).

Obviously, given their economic circumstances and religious belief in modesty, the conversion of an existing building to a chapel was the most expedient course of action, and it was said that 'as we convert souls so we convert barns, both to the Glory of God'. In most cases a congregation would have already registered a place where they met as 'a chapel' – often it was where they had met secretly during the times when they were doing so illegally. The most popular candidate for adaptation to a chapel was a farm barn, for all that was urgently required was a secure clean place, a meeting-house with a worshipful atmosphere. Thus the period from the Act of Toleration in 1689 to the late 1700s is sometimes called the period of the 'barn-chapels' – also known as 'the little granaries of God'. This is a more telling description than it at first appears, for it implies that the core of Dissent was in the rural areas, and that the spiritual and historic home of Nonconformity was in the countryside and in the hearts of the country folk rather than the town dwellers.

CHAPTER 3

The Eighteenth Century: Schisms and Splinters

T hroughout the eighteenth century Nonconformity grew and spread across the whole of Wales, eventually achieving a blanket coverage of all areas, with growth in the north occurring considerably more slowly than in the increasingly-industrialized and more populous south. The population of Wales was itself growing: in 1700 it was about 400,000, but by 1800 this had increased to almost 600,000, though this was nothing compared with what was to happen in the years 1800 to 1900. Although Nonconformity was growing, it was patchy and subject to spurts due to some specific stimulus, like a revival. The greatest of these stimuli was the development of Methodism, which affected all of the other Nonconformist denominations from the middle years of the century, and created a foundation for the massive expansion of Nonconformity in the nineteenth century.

Methodism is associated in the popular mind with John Wesley in England, but it developed quite independently and earlier in Wales, as a spontaneous Welsh movement that owed nothing to its English counterpart. With Methodism in the vanguard, the Nonconformists in the eighteenth century steadily consolidated their position and built upon an increasingly-firm foundation. But it was also a century of upheaval and troubles, one of 'spurts and schisms'. Wales was 'a maelstrom of religious opinions, with the most fanciful and extravagant views being propagated alongside the sober and cultivated . . .'. In the time of persecution there had been general unity, but now there were open clashes over doctrinal matters and interpretation of Scripture. As the various denominations began to till their theological ground, contentious and divisive issues surfaced – discordant interpretations of the Bible, rupturing of congregations, sharp animosities. It was a kind of scriptural civil war, and it led to many breakaway congregations who called themselves 'the splinters' and went off to build splinter chapels of their own. Given the high degree of independence of spirit of the Nonconformists, their independence of action, and the passion of the Enthusiasts, perhaps this was not surprising. As the century wore on matters of religion were the intellectual meat-and-drink of the day. A major revival broke out in 1735, and others followed, each stoking up the fire of religious passion.

The Methodists' activity was concentrated on the very same issue that had so exercised the Puritans and Dissenters – preaching – coupled with a return to the Welsh-language issue that continued to plague the Church, and a pattern begins to emerge during this period that links an awakening nationalism rooted in the Welsh language to Nonconformity. Methodism was an out-and-out evangelical movement that wanted to save souls and initially cared less for having a church building in which to do so. Itinerant preachers roamed far and wide, their horses burdened with portable pulpits – used even by John Wesley – from which to exhort the Gospel. These sermonizers had a remarkable ability to communicate with those who could not read, and those who heard them fell under the enthralling oratorial power of these preachers, who brought the Bible to life:

Preaching was the bellows through which the divine wind of Heaven was blown to raise the emotional temperature of the hearers. Only in the volcanic heat created by inspired pulpit oratory could the stubborn heart be melted by the overpowering emotions of guilt, fear, shame, anguish, hope, joy, and certainty, and so surrender itself to the great decision.

Glanmor Williams, The Welsh and their Religion, *University of Wales Press, 1991*

The preachers were the master allegorists of the day. They were theologians, poets, philosophers, and their sermons were dramas – the preacher was playwright and actor, and brought a touch of the theatre into the chapels. A single example of preaching will suffice to demonstrate how direct and powerfully expressive metaphors were employed to galvanize an audience, and make the Gospel real for those who heard it. This is part of a sermon based on Jeremiah 6.29, delivered by the legendary one-eyed Revd Christmas Evans to iron-workers and foundrymen:

The furnace which the patriarchs had was a small one and its bellows too weak to create sufficient heat to melt the ore. But the furnace built on Sinai belonged to Abraham and Company, and the deeds of that company extended deep into the seams of Israel. And when the furnace was built on the Hill of Golgotha the God of Eternity decided to take charge of all the territories, to sink shafts and open levels to all the seams of Eden and to take down that old furnace built on Sinai, and to open a new forge and a new furnace on Calvary. . . . The bellows is the Gospel, the Word of Truth is the ore, the death of Christ is the furnace, and His eternal love is the fiery fuel which melts that ore, and the Holy Ghost is the agent who supervises the undertaking – it is He who looks after the furnace, it is He who runs the ore in to the moulds of faith and repentance, and it is He who takes the iron through the mills of Eternal Truth.

T.M. Bassett, The Welsh Baptists, *Ilston House Press, 1977*

The chapel-building frenzy was primarily driven by the passion of the preachers to erect their Bethels and Tabernacles throughout Wales. In their evangelizing they were

4 'Kings of the Pulpit': three of the greatest of the Welsh preachers, whose passionate sermonizing could bring a congregation to a state of religious ecstasy and frenzy, and whose appearance could fill chapels to overflowing – they often had to preach to the multitudes on hillsides. In the centre is the legendary one-eyed giant, the Revd Christmas Evans of Anglesey, minister at Capel Cildwrn (see 5, 6, 7); on the left is John Elias and on the right W. Williams o'r Wern.

collecting souls for salvation and money for chapels. These were exceptional individuals possessed of great stamina, fierce conviction, and imaginative oratorial skills (4). Their sermons were vivid and poetic, full of clarity of expression and fresh immediacy, and especially effective in a nation particularly susceptible to this kind of spellbinding narrative.

WESLEY AND THE SERMONS IN STONE

A century after religious Toleration in 1689, Wales prepared to enter the nineteenth century as a very different country. Certainly the Nonconformists were busy sprouting chapels in almost every county, but they were as yet incidental to the changes that were wrenching Wales from its agrarian base and imposing a massive industrialization – with all the cataclysmic forces that attend such dramatic realignments. Heavy industry like copper and iron smelting began on a large scale, especially during the Seven Years War of 1756–63, growing near the coalfields in the

5 From cottage-worship to growing chapel. The genesis of Capel Cildwrn, Llangefni, Ang., from a tiny house where the congregation met . . .

south and by 1780 the southern valleys were crowned by a dark band of ironworks that spread out from Merthyr and Dowlais. By the 1780s an equally significant change was affecting the north through copper mining and slate quarrying, and whole new communities like Blaenau Ffestiniog appeared where there had been none before. Towns and localities became synonymous with various aspects of industry, with Merthyr Tydfil and Dowlais identified with iron, the Rhondda with coal, Penarth, Barry, Cardiff and Newport with shipping Welsh products, Llanelli with tin, and Neath was known as 'Copperopolis'. Such industrialization required improved transportation. The atrocious roads were repaired and extended, a canal system built, and the railways were steaming towards Wales.

The country which had been isolated from the rest of Britain and the world was now subject to all the turmoil that came with such rapid change, and the vagaries of market forces. The population began to grow very quickly, immigration from the farming communities to the industrial belt occurred alongside the arrival of workers from England and Ireland. There was serious civil disturbance and major rioting throughout

17

6   7

. . . to the first modest chapel (6) which was eventually extended to create a two-storey chapel (7) with a large gallery to accommodate the capacity congregations who came to hear Revd Christmas Evans preach. He lived in the small minister's house attached to the chapel, complaining about the low ceilings – understandable for a preacher who was nearly 7 ft tall.

the 1790s, mostly over the appalling working and living conditions and the lack of food – malnutrition and starvation were not at all uncommon. The industries expanded and became hungrier than ever for men and material, consuming both at a furious pace.

All these forces affected, and were affected by the Nonconformists. They were by nature responsive and mobile, and took advantage of both the increasing population and the excitement of stirring religious revivals to secure new converts, who in turn became informal evangelists and drew others, by example, to the chapels. Chapel-building began to increase, especially after the late 1780s, and rapidly accelerated after 1815 with the congregations from that period onwards becoming increasingly ambitious about what kind of new chapel they would build. The Nonconformists became increasingly confident and their chapels began to have a central role in every Welsh community. In the coming nineteenth century this would be massively amplified and reflected in the kind of buildings they would erect. In the century that led up to the eruption of the Methodists' separation from the Church (1811) the fragility of early Dissent completely disappeared. Their chapels became larger, better appointed, and the era of converting barns and cowhouses very quickly evaporated. Congregations wanted new and purpose-built chapels that were 'fitted-up proper' and to specification. Daniel Owen (himself a Methodist preacher), writing in 1880, looked back in his novel *Gwen Tomos* on such a modestly ambitious congregation:

Tan y Fron Chapel was like every other chapel to be found in the Welsh countryside . . . it had no architectural form, and did credit only to the most ordinary of stonemasons. The faithful brethren who built it gave the design but a moment's consideration. The only thing that mattered to them was its size, the number of feet that they could make it longer or wider than old Talyllyn barn. Having decided that point the only other consideration was that it should be a suitable shelter for the worship of God. It consisted of four plain walls, four high windows, a door on one side wall, and a roof of slates. Inside, at one end, was a pulpit, reached by a steep stair, and a narrow Big Pew whose occupants suffered from stiff necks through gazing up at the preacher. To overcome this they slouched in their seats and became permanently round-shouldered. . . . The seats themselves were mostly just moveable forms, with no backs, and on these the congregation, mostly elderly folk, sat without complaint. Indeed, they considered the seating arrangements to be excellent. Later, some members asked to be allowed to have proper pews, but this request was considered to be an extravagant luxury. It was only after they had agreed to install the pews at their own expense that they were allowed to have them.

These chapels grew from domestic meetings in ordinary houses, and the growth of the chapel from those humble beginnings into capacious 'temples' is shown in three drawings from the history of Capel Cildwrn, Llangefni, Ang., the first Baptist cause in Anglesey. The original Tŷ Cildwrn was built around 1750, but grew into a simple chapel-and-house, and in 1846 to a much-enlarged version, but still on the same site. Both the chapel and the hardy tree (5, 6, 7) depicted in the drawings are still there, but only the tree is growing.

When the congregations designed their chapels, they had only to look over their shoulder to what they had left behind for an idea about what they were to build, and they modelled their chapel on the kind of practical and flexible preaching-space that a barn had provided for them. There was no central authority to direct their work or legislate on their design, for the Nonconformists had no Church Commissioners to instruct them. There would never be any such authority to create a 'chapel style' for the Congregationalists, Independents, Baptists, Unitarians or Calvinistic Methodists.

The Wesleyan Methodists, however, began to develop some firmer ideas about chapel architecture. John Wesley was particularly interested in this issue, and had strong views and well-articulated ideas about how the 'preaching-houses' should look. Wesley's own instructions were quite clear, and based on what he considered to be sound architectural practice. He believed that all preaching-houses should be on an octagonal plan (which he thought 'best for the voice, and most commodious') though he thought the square-plan was an alternative, with a rectangle less desirable; that there should be lots of windows 'with sashes opening downwards'; that the pulpit 'shall be a square projection with a wide seat behind, not a tub-pulpit'; and that 'there should not be pews, and no back to the seats . . . and [these should] be parted in the middle to divide the men from the women'; and that 'lodgings be provided for the preacher'. Wesley wanted the preaching-houses to be 'plain and decent, but not more expensive than absolutely necessary'. Often the planning was intended to recall the earliest Christian churches and encourage similar simplicity of character – when Tennyson saw the basilica at Trier, Germany, he thought it would make 'an ideal Methodist chapel'.

This practical and reasonable approach was certainly followed by many Wesleyan Methodists, but Wesley's common-sense views on a building style that was neat, simple, and economically-built from local materials was the approach being followed without his advice in Wales by all the Nonconformists in this period. Its principles were kept in place and respected until the onslaught of 'architecture by architects' which began in earnest in the middle 1800s.

Of the two options open to Wesleyan Methodists, the square-plan was favoured over the octagon (which was rather more difficult to built on account of the more costly roof), but the common rectangular barn-plan was by far the commonest, with a gable-end facade. The vernacular side-wall-facade so reminiscent of Welsh farmhouse architecture was not as significant a part of the architectural genetics of Methodism as it was the other Nonconformist denominations, and the Wesleyans were quick to adopt a building style that from the outset had reflections of Georgian, Classic and especially Gothic architecture.

The inevitable effect of revival activity and reflection about what chapels were to be was to spur chapel-building, because the chapel was the home of preaching. Preachers were a driving and powerful force and the histories of the period are awash with them as the most effective 'movers and shakers' of the century. The Methodist revival and the religious renaissance of Wales could never have succeeded without the oratorical ability of these men to capture the hearts and imaginations of their listeners. Daniel Rowland (1713–90), an ordained Church minister, and Howell Harris (1714–73), were the acknowledged charismatic leaders of Methodism in Wales, and their respective homes at Llangeitho, Card., and Trefeca, Brec., were the twin 'Meccas of Methodism' in Wales. They together dominated the religious landscape, and the result was an increasing neglect of the centres of the Established Church – St David's, Bangor and Llandaff – as congregations turned to the Nonconformist 'holy places' like Llangeitho, Bala and Trefeca. People turned from what they saw as a cold Church to the embrace of a warm chapel.

Wesley preached many sermons in Wales, mostly in the open air – it was said that 'the architecture of his chapel was that of nature itself – the grass its floor, the trees its columns, the sky its roof, a rock or hillock was its pulpit' (George Dolby, *The Architectural Expression of Methodism*, Epworth Press, 1964). But Wesleyan Methodism did not flourish in Wales until the nineteenth century, when a vast influx of people from England moved into the industrialized south, and inflated the numbers attending the Methodist chapels. By the time Wesley came to Wales the Wesleyan Methodists in England had already been busy building chapels, while the

Calvinistic Methodists built their first denominational chapel in Wales at Groes-wen, near Caerphilly, in 1742. The building was possibly designed by William Edwards, who built Libanus in Morriston in 1782.

The Methodist chapels were not independent churches, but overflow preaching houses of the Established Church. The Methodists did not call their buildings chapels, in case they would be seen as 'small churches for worship', and very rarely called them meeting-houses as that word associated them with the separatist Nonconformists. Wesley rigidly held to the phrase 'Methodist Preaching-houses'. Other chapels were, however, completely separatist in their actions, and thus are precursors of the Welsh Methodists' complete separation from the Church in 1811.

As the eighteenth century drew towards its last years, the Nonconformists were increasingly successful in their quest for converts, and their chapels became increasingly unable to accommodate the congregations. The average lifespan for a chapel building was less than twenty years, and the average cost in the period 1790–1810 for a chapel to accommodate about 250 people was below £200, though one was built in 1786 for as little as £60, complete and 'with the key in the door'. (In 1825 the congregation at Swyddfynnon also managed to build their new chapel for £60, an increase over the tender figure of £45. It measured a modest 27 ft by 18 ft.) A new chapel was sometimes a far too substantial investment and this drove the congregations to attempt constant patching-up and making-do and extension of the chapel to make it last as long as possible. There were ebbs and flows of revivalism, and of chapel-building; during one of the quiet times some observers thought that Nonconformity was a spent force, not realizing that it was resting, not sleeping. Lewis Morris, writing in 1757, could not have imagined how prophetic were his comments when he wrote:

Religion in Wales is quite out of taste, it is such an old-fashioned thing. I am positive that if Mohammed had some daring fellows to preach here he would gain ground immediately – or any merry religion like that. And if Sadler's Wells and the Playhouses could be brought in as branches of the new religion it would have an abundance of converts and take extremely well.

Lewis Morris, 1757, in T.M. Bassett, The Welsh Baptists, *Ilston House Press, 1977*

This was a startling prediction, to be realized in the years spanning the turn of the century, when the combination of preaching by 'daring fellows' like Christmas Evans and Williams o'r Wern, in their new playhouse style of chapel, would lead to a vast 'abundance of converts' to Nonconformity, if not Mohammedanism.

CHAPTER 4

Barn-chapels: 'The Little Granaries of God'

. . . the earliest 'Bethels', with their high gables, plain whitewashed walls and roofs of thick slate or thin stone, are evidence of a native instinct for combining utility and beauty. See them on a summer's day with their gleaming whitewash, against which are limned the dark yews or cypresses which line the stone-paved pathways to their little cemeteries, with moss-grown headstones, and you will agree with me.

Michael Llewellyn, The Sand in the Glass, *John Murray, 1943*

There are no surviving chapel buildings from the 1600s other than Maesyronnen, and even examples from 1700 to 1800 are quite rare. The revivals and the creation of the splinter chapels caused the demolition and replacement of many chapels from that century. There are, however, some examples that can still be seen and viewed in comparison with Maesyronnen: two are still on their original lonely sites (Capel Beiliheulog and Capel Newydd); the other (Capel Pen-rhiw) is literally 'of museum quality'.

Capel Beiliheulog (or Bailihalog) Independent chapel (Plates 4, 5) is hard to find, hidden deep in the twisting lanes of the Nantoffeiriaid valley near Gwenddwr, Brec., but the difficulty in getting to it is a useful experience in remembering the faith and hardiness of early Dissenters to gather in remote seclusion. The chapel was built in 1740, though the congregation had been meeting here secretly in the days of Dissenter persecution. In terms of its site and exterior it exudes an untouched quality, though the interior was somewhat altered in the early nineteenth century. The facade is symmetrical, but the door is on the gable-end, with the pulpit facing it on the opposite wall, an arrangement that would not be common in Wales for another seventy years, but which appears in another small chapel, very similar to Beiliheulog, the Methodists' Earlswood, Mon., of 1791.

Pen-y-garn, near Pontypool, Mon., Baptist, 1727 (8), is a larger structure, to accommodate a congregation of about 300. The side-wall-facade has the addition of a later porch, but is otherwise generally unchanged. The worshippers for the nearby industrializing Pontypool were said to 'so respect their little Tabernacle that they removed their dirty boots before they entered'. Services in this period were daytime events, the

8 An early purpose-built chapel of 1727, Pen-y-garn, Pontypool. Chapels that have survived from the 1700s are rare as successive religious revivals swelled membership and the old chapel was then demolished and replaced with a new one. Pen-y-garn retains the old pattern of the facade being one of the long side walls.

Sunday focus moving to evenings only later in the nineteenth century with the advent of better lighting and heating. Services were of several hours duration, and Pen-y-garn's congregation, like many others, brought food with them for lunch and tea.

The chapel contains a modest gallery, reached by a stone spiral staircase. Pen-y-garn is on a far more substantial scale than those chapels described previously, but the introduction of the gallery was not a feature restricted to town chapels with growing congregations. Rural chapel-builders of the period often planned their chapels to have a roof high enough to permit the later insertion of a gallery. Some congregations that later needed a gallery but had a chapel with a low roof simply dug out the floor to get the extra head-room.

The siting of these small country chapels is often inspired. The Baptist cause at Capel-y-ffin, Brec., in 1737, tucked their chapel into a steep hill that rose like a theatrical back-drop behind the building. This chapel was spacious in comparison with that of the cramped worshippers and minister who inhabited the little Independent chapel at Gwernogle, Carm. (9), in the depths of the Brechfa forest, which reveals its simple cruck-and-thatch roof construction, and tiny scale. The Nonconformists were

9 The remains of a tiny rural combination of chapel and minister's house of cruck-and-thatch construction, in the depths of the Brechfa Forest, at Gwernogle, Carm., built in the mid-1700s. Many congregations worshipped in equally austere chapels until the great revivals of the nineteenth century overtook them and they built anew.

also building larger chapels: Bethlehem, St Clears, Carm., Independent, 1768, was a substantial square-plan chapel (altered in the nineteenth century).

Capel Newydd, Independent, 1770 (Plate 3), at Nanhoron on the Llŷn Peninsula in North Wales, is a conversion of a rough fieldstone barn. As at Maesyronnen, the facade is the long side wall with two entrance doors – with an older central filled-in doorway surmounted by a gabled window inserted at the time of conversion, to illuminate the pulpit area within. Although the interior has had some early nineteenth-century alterations, the overall sense is of unspoiled originality.

The pulpit – which was acquired from a disused local church – is high, and the whole interior is divided into deep wooden box pews with hinged doors, all raised above the beaten-earth floors on large lumps of stone. A narrow aisle running the full east–west axis gives on to the pews and the simple tiered benches set against the west gable-end wall. Simple candle sconces flank the pulpit, which is also lit by equally plain candlesticks to light the Bible (in this period evening services were unusual, but the candles might be lit on gloomy winter afternoons); there are also two turned-wood candelabra on pulley-ropes attached to the ceiling, which has exposed beams. There are two unusual features of this chapel, both nevertheless being quite practical. The first is the pair of long-handled wooden shovels, kept in the Big Seat area, that are actually the collection plates, long enough to reach the length of the deep pews. The other feature is to be seen hanging above the western doorway: an *elor* or coffin-carrier, surely a stark intimation of mortality and the focus of many a sermon.

A similar coffin-carrier roosts in the rafters of Capel Pen-rhiw, another barn-conversion that opened as a chapel in 1777 at Drefach-Felindre, Carm. (10), but no longer resides there. It was carefully demolished and even more carefully rebuilt at St Fagans, near Cardiff, at the Museum of Welsh Life, the open-air museum of Welsh buildings. During the meticulous re-creation of Pen-rhiw, the interior was also fully restored and reinstalled. The random-rubble walls are covered with a heavy coat of whitewash, in fine contrast with the stone roof tiles installed by the museum in returning the building to its original appearance. The exterior, like that of Maesyronnen and Capel Newydd, is symmetrical, and gives a clear indication of the interior layout. The chapel is set in a small courtyard with low earth birms which have stone seats set into them, which were used by the overflow congregations during the preaching festivals of the period. Pen-rhiw at one point looked even more like a Welsh 'long-house', when it had a small stable or house attached to the gable-end.

The interior of Capel Pen-rhiw (11) shows the slow transition of chapel interior design. In comparison with the oldest model, Maesyronnen, this chapel clearly shows a greater attention to detail, more care in the assembly of the components, and more thought about the needs of the congregation. The original hay-loft was converted some years after the ground floor had been completed, in response to an enlarging congregation, and properly furnished with built-in pews. This was a strategy adopted by a number of chapels as it increased accommodation while avoiding the greater expense of complete demolition and rebuilding. There was no shred of doubt among these congregations that a massive religious revival was coming, and they planned for it.

The ground-floor of Pen-rhiw shows pews that were the 'property' of families, who paid for them to be made and installed. Such subscription seating becomes more common in chapels as the century wears on, and were a standard feature of chapels in the nineteenth century as social hierarchies developed within the chapels. Two pews with arcaded tops flank the pulpit at Pen-rhiw, and were for the deaconate, the elders of the chapel, and the Big Seat arrangement is now well established as significant feature of the interior architecture. The floor is of compressed earth, but at Pen-rhiw has been boarded over in front of the pulpit. Although the Nonconformists never formally ascribed 'holiness' to places, or venerated objects as 'worshipful', they constantly referred to 'respect' for their place of worship, and the need for 'seemliness', so a special treatment for the pulpit and communion area was appropriate in the unpretentious and highly functional interior of Pen-rhiw chapel.

10 One of the finest preserved of the barn-chapels, the 'little granaries of God', Capel Pen-rhiw was originally at Drefach-Felindre in West Wales, but is now at the Museum of Welsh Life, St Fagans, Cardiff, where it has been rebuilt and meticulously restored. The chapel was a barn until 1777, when it became a simple temple, its hayloft being later converted into a gallery.

11 The pulpit and 'Big Seat' for deacons at Capel Pen-rhiw, the minister backlit by the central window of the facade. The pulpit, ever the focal point, was raised when the gallery was created, to ensure that the minister could be seen by all, and he could see them.

12 Chapels were far more than places for worship on
Sundays: they were multi-functional buildings and their role
as schools was central to many communities – many
eventually added schoolroom annexes to their main chapel
buildings. Here at Maesberllan, Talach-ddu, Brec., a specific
area of the ground floor was designed as a small schoolroom,
with a fireplace, contained within the chapel.

A particular feature of Pen-rhiw is the history of the building as a social and
educational centre for the community, as well as being the chapel. Many chapels,
especially in rural Wales, fulfilled multiple roles, and Pen-rhiw is an early example
of how chapels were eventually to become the most important building for the local
population. It served as chapel and school, and was therefore in constant daily use,
not only on Sunday for worship. It was 'open all hours' for children by day and adult
education classes in the evenings, and for Sunday School after the services on the
Sabbath. (In country chapels one often finds features that reflect this maximization of
the use of the building, especially as a schoolroom, even well into the nineteenth
century, by which time discrete school buildings were common. Maesberllan, Talach-
ddu, Brec., of 1805 and 1835 (12), has a distinct area of the main floor set aside as
the school part of the chapel, with a fireplace set into the wall of a purpose-designed
enclosure.)

Some chapels survived long enough to be captured by the camera, and their ghosts

13

A nineteenth-century photographer captured two early chapels before they were demolished, showing quite how simple and unassuming they were, indistinguishable from the cottages of the countryside in the 1700s. Thatched Capel y Bryngwyn (13) was at Abergele, Denbs., built *c.* 1720, and Bwlch-y-rhiw (14) at Llandovery, Carm., about the same period.

14

15   **16**

Thatch was replaced by stone and slate roofs, but a few examples have survived – The Pales (15) is a Quaker meeting-house near Llandegley, Rad., built in 1716. Capel y Crynwyr (16), near Pontrobert, *c*. 1750, also retains the reticence of chapels in this era, anxious to avoid any showiness or even to declare themselves to be churches.

show us quite how small and humble these meeting-houses were, while emphasizing how reluctant the Nonconformists were to abandon the grass-roots vernacular traditions of their buildings. Capel y Bryngwyn (13) was a tiny mud-walled thatched meeting-house near Abergele, Denbs., around 1715, while the Bwlch-y-rhiw Baptists met in their small chapel (14) near Llandovery, Carm., in the same period. Mud walls and a thatched roof were used to build the Baptist chapel at Ty'ndonnen, Llŷn, as late as 1786. A few others have survived, even though there have been inevitable alterations, but the thatched Quaker meeting-house named The Pales, near Llandegley, Rad., built 1716 (15), is largely intact, and the later Capel y Crynwyr, Dolobran, Pontrobert, Mont., Independent, *c*. 1750 (16), is indistinguishable from domestic architecture of this period.

CHAPTER 5

The Early Nineteenth Century: A Hint of 'Architecture'

Despised by architects, ignored by guide books, too briefly mentioned in directories, these variegated conventicles are witnesses to the taste of industrial Britain. They try to ape nothing. They were anxious not to look like the Church, which held them in contempt; nor like a house, for they were places of worship; nor like a theatre, for they were sacred piles. They succeeded in looking like what they are – chapels, so that the most unobservant traveller can tell a chapel from any other building on the street.

John Betjeman, First and Last Loves, *John Murray, 1969*

In 1808 a tide of revival washed across Wales, but the single event most associated with the eruption of religious fervour, and the explosion of chapel-building, was the 1811 separation of the Welsh Methodists from the Anglican Church, for they were now certain that the Church would never accommodate them – theologically or physically. A rapidly-rising number of Methodists refused to go to church for worship at all in the face of such animosity, and the result was a speedy increase in the congregations at the Methodist preaching-houses, which were becoming inadequate. If this is combined with the growth of population in Wales, it was a recipe for a pressure that became intolerable. When the Methodists finally left the Church they were popularly (or unpopularly) viewed as Nonconformist separatists along with the Baptists, Congregationalists and Unitarians, a perception they had been at pains to avoid. All the denominations were affected by the Methodist actions, and the result was a new round of revivalism and the urgent need to build new chapels.

The Methodists were the particular target of unforgiving Anglican scorn, and an English visitor to Wales was to write that on a country road he saw: 'A field of grain on one side, and a chapel on the other: what better symbols of poverty and meanness could one find than Oats and Methodism' (Michael Llewellyn, *The Sand in the Glass*, John Murray, 1943).

PENIEL, TREMADOG

Before 'architecture' arrived in Wales it sent a herald to announce that it was coming. In 1810 Peniel (17, Plate 6), a beautiful small chapel, was erected on the instructions of William Madocks, entrepreneur and MP for Boston, in his new town of Tremadog. It owed nothing to the vernacular traditions of Welsh Nonconformity, and its appearance was that of a Classical temple planted in the rugged landscape of the north: Athens and Rome had come to Caernarfonshire.

Among Madocks' elegant and finely-proportioned collection of new buildings Peniel chapel was a sharp contrast, a crisp square-plan preaching-house with a gable-end Tuscan portico thrusting forward, the triangular pediment with wheel-window supported by two substantial columns, to create a deep porch for protection from the weather. The flat-stucco painted finish of the Classical facade is in delicate contrast with the rough-dressed fieldstone side walls.

Peniel is a strikingly pretty building, and its unusual appearance on a prominent site must have created a lasting impression on those who saw it, or heard about it, though it was not immediately copied by other congregations, for few had the wherewithal to pay for such a building. Nevertheless Peniel was highly influential for some of its features were to be widely integrated into chapel design throughout Wales. It is implausible that anyone in Wales but Madocks could or would have built such a well-designed chapel with such Classical references, for Peniel, refined and elegant as it was, was unique in the country. No other chapel in Wales of those years, or the years immediately before, could match the grander preaching-houses already built in England. The diminutive scale and domestic associations of the Welsh chapels remained a constant for many decades. Peniel was the precursor of the Classical style revival in Wales that was to change profoundly the nature of chapel architecture. And 'architecture' it was, for it was inspired by an existing building, not in Athens or Rome, but in London. St Paul's Church of 1638 at Covent Garden, London (18), by Inigo Jones (1573–1653) is one of the finest complete Classically-inspired churches in London, once described as 'the handsomest barn in England', though it was certainly not a conversion like the barn-chapels of Wales. Peniel may have been the first example of 'interloper architecture' in Wales, but perhaps the lack of obvious Anglican Gothic references, coupled with the fame and Welsh name of 'Henygo' Jones helped the design of the chapel gain more ready acceptance.

Peniel may have been a surprise physical import from England, but it seems very likely that John Wesley's ideas about chapel architecture were known among the Methodists, both the minority Wesleyans and the majority Calvinists. The form of

17   **18**

'Architecture' came to chapel-building in 1810, and marked a significant break with the side-wall facade traditional chapel and its reflection of vernacular traditions. Peniel, Tremadog, Caern., brought themes from Classical architecture and displayed them on a gable-end facade, a design that was new and in due course would powerfully affect those who were building chapels in increasing numbers. Peniel (17) was highly original in Wales, but itself based on St Paul's Church, Covent Garden, of 1638 (18).

Wesley's own chapel at City Road, London, of 1778, a gable-end facade building in a light Georgian style, with an 1810 Greek Doric porch, may also have been known in Wales and been a working model. Although a building not without faults, it became the accepted basic design for Methodist chapels, in part because of the 1790 Methodist Conference declaring that 'All preaching-houses to be built in the future shall be upon the same plan as the City Road, London'. Some congregations were to adhere to this while others did not, but the general appearance of the five-bayed gable-end Georgian facade was highly influential and widely adopted in Wales by all the Nonconformist denominations, the Welsh Baptist chapel at Denbigh, 1836, being the closest facsimile (49).

The interior of Peniel is as significant and as surprising as its exterior, with a raked floor to improve the congregation's view of the pulpit, which is placed against the western gable-wall, opposite the facade's entrance doors. The present gallery is a later addition. Peniel showed the way to a new kind of chapel, and its interior form was eventually adopted as the standard format for virtually every chapel built in Wales after 1850. In addition to the obvious design change from a vernacular recollection to Classical references, the interior reorients the congregation. The reference of which they would perhaps have been unaware was to the 'auditory churches' of Christopher Wren (1632–1723), in London, a design specification that Wren promoted as being particularly good for acoustics – vital to any preacher. The result in Wales was to turn the building around, and pack in more people by putting them in serried ranks facing the pulpit, rather than in a fan-array. The effect was to change the chapel from a meeting-house into an auditorium, and the congregation from a gathered church into an audience.

Madocks had already built an Anglican church at Tremadog in 1806, a gloomy spired Gothic work atop a tump of earth and rock, then built Peniel close by. The Bishop of Bangor was surprised at this lavish provision for the Nonconformists, and complained to Madocks, who adroitly replied that the church was 'On solid rock, and the chapel built only on the sand'. Both church and chapel still stand on their differing foundations.

Peniel, in 1810, was a clear indication of what was to come in the increasing 'architecturalization' of chapels. The building has many historic references, with details like the wheel-window in the pediment, Classical columns and capitals, together with smooth stucco surfaces, contrasting coloured trim, etc., all being traceable to a design history completely alien to Wales. It also demonstrates a higher quality of craftsmanship, an emphasis on the glamour and showiness of the gable-end facade, and above all, it was carefully designed as a purpose-built chapel. In the same year that Peniel was planted on the Tremadog sands, the Quakers in Aberystwyth were drawing the building conversion tradition to a close, turning an old coach-house and estate office into their chapel. The Friends Meeting-house (now the Unitarian Meeting-house), Aberystwyth, 1810, is one of the very last examples of the tradition of adaptive re-use (along with the conversion of the old slaughter-house at Bagillt in 1815). The present facade dates from about 1906 (when the Unitarians bought it), a bold anthropomorphic design – possibly by John Hartland of Cardiff (165). After 1810–15 it is rare to find a chapel being created in Wales by any other means than it being purpose-built from the outset. The Nonconformists were not fettered with regulations and the delays that the Church faced in building a new house for worship, and they were very speedy in erecting a new chapel where the need was felt. Congregations were succeeding in getting sites given to them by landowners who were becoming more sympathetic to the hardworking and reliable Nonconformists. Most country congregations retained their loyalty to the old barn references in their buildings, recalling the places they still thought of as their spiritual homes, and many of these chapels went through successive rebuildings, retaining this design, but increasing the size. The plaque on Glandŵr chapel in Carmarthenshire, tells the typical story of their organic development: 'Built 1712, rebuilt and enlarged 1774, rebuilt and enlarged 1836, renewed and improved 1876. O.R. Owen, Minister'.

However, several important changes to the appearance of the chapels occur in the period from about 1775 to about 1825, the most significant being the slow departure of the chapel design away from the replication of the farm-barn tradition. The chapels get much bigger, even if still retaining the side wall format, with a strong horizontal design emphasis though there are now notable vertical features like double-height round-headed sash windows (Llwynrhydowen (Plate 10) and Bethlehem Green (37) are examples). As a counterpoint to this, the horizontal emphasis is played off against a design that stresses strong vertical bands and bays on the chapels that have gable-end facades. As we enter the second decade of the nineteenth century the number of clear references to a classicism imported from England and the history of architecture begin to increase dramatically.

By 1820 a widespread, simple but very significant change had occurred in the appearance of the chapels. Even if they retained their allegiance to the farm-barn tradition, the congregations now seemed to want to make sure that their meeting-houses were seen as chapels, as places of worship, and to set them apart from vernacular expressions. They wanted a feature or a form that would serve readily to identify their building as a church, an easily-read symbol that would instantly set the chapel buildings apart from the domestic traditions, but which would also signal the beginning of a complete detachment from those traditions. They employed a highly effective device to accomplish their aims: they made the windows round-headed.

Round-headed windows were a feature of the facade of John Wesley's City Road Chapel in London (1778), but the other London antecedent was to be found in the popular city churches of Christopher Wren. In these beautifully-scaled churches Wren seems virtually to have invented an influential tradition which held that 'a worshipful atmosphere' (as the Nonconformists called it), or the 'ecclesiastical character' of a building could be created by the use of round-headed windows. Before 1810 in Wales there were chapels with round-headed doorways, but by the end of the first decade of the nineteenth century the chapel-builders applied the round-heads to windows and doorways alike, often mixing them with square-heads in clever counterpoint on the same facade. This simple device immediately created a 'chapel identity' for a building, but it was also a sign that the chapels were moving away from their vernacular history. The Nonconformists were declaring themselves more forthrightly and robustly than heretofore, leaving observers in no doubt that their chapel was a house of God, and could no longer be mistaken for a barn, and strong symmetrical designs characterise the facades of these chapels.

In the period from 1810 to 1840, especially in rural areas, there is a slow but steady transition to rectangular-plan gable-end chapels. Many were small and still almost indistinguishable from houses, drawing little attention to themselves as chapels, but the growing or more ambitious congregations that chose to continue the side-wall-facade chapels simply kept to that design, but increased the size. Pencader, Carm., Independent, 1827 (19), Capel y Carn, Bowstreet, Card.,

19 Ambitious and expanding congregations in the early nineteenth century were loyal to the old side-wall facade pattern of the first single-storey 'barn-chapels', but they needed bigger buildings. The solution was to double the height and install galleries around three sides of the interior walls. Pencader, Carm., did this in 1827, with a fieldstone facade very much in keeping with rural building traditions. Many congregations integrated a schoolroom or permanent dwelling for their minister into the design of the chapel, as to the left of the main chapel here at Pencader.

Methodist, 1833 (by William Jones for £502, with a later detached chapel-house) (111, 112, Plate 18), and the spacious and galleried Llwynrhydowen, Card., Unitarian, 1834 (Plate 10), with its hipped roof and fine scale are all excellent examples.

A few congregations foreswore both long-wall and gable-end, and still built square-plan chapels. These were said to be easier to preach in as 'oratorial space', but there may also have been another reason: in their careful reading and interpretation of the Scripture they saw the reference that 'The City of the Lord shall lie Foursquare, and the Breadth shall be no Greater than the Length' (21 Rev. 16). Square-plan chapels with pyramidal roofs in smaller towns and villages are not unusual, like Salem, Llandovery, Carm., Independent, 1829 (20); Bozrah, Pen-sarn, Ang., Calvinistic Methodist, 1864, with a square courtyard flanked by the minister's chapel-house and the schoolroom on either side (21); Capel Ifan, Llannerch-y-medd,

20 Many preachers favoured chapels that had a square plan and said that it made for good oratorical space and that they were easier to preach in. Salem, Llandovery, is an 1829 example, with a pyramidal roof . . .

Ang., Congregationalist, 1870. Quite substantial square-plan chapels are to be found in the countryside like Yr Hen Gapel Ffynnon, Llanddewi Velfrey, Pemb., Baptist, *c*. 1770 and 1850 (22).

The rural chapels of the early nineteenth century were not consistent in the use of materials, and there are many variations usually accounted for by the ready availability of some local material, such as slate. Some chapels were built of random fieldstone that was lightly dressed, such as Caerfarchell, Pemb., Calvinistic Methodist, 1827 (where it was reported that 'horses' skulls were laid into the foundations, to kill the echo') (23), but at Ainon, Llanuwchllyn, Mer., Baptist, 1840 (24), the walls are little more than large rough boulders. The farmhouse tradition of rendering the facade with a heavy whitewashing or limewashing was a popular treatment, neatly evening out the very rough surface of imperfect fieldstone. This was carried on to the chapels and gave a uniformity of appearance in the countryside that joined, as of old, chapel and barn alike. This whitewashing tradition carries into the mid-century, after which very few

21

... as is (21) Bozrah, Pen-sarn, Ang., built in 1864 on a square plot of land, with a minister's house to the left of the courtyard and a substantial schoolroom and storehouse to the right. A large and imposing Pembrokeshire version, Yr Hen Gapel Ffynnon (22), crests a hillside at Llanddewi Velfrey, built 1770 and rebuilt 1850.

22

23 Congregations often built the chapels themselves, carrying stone from quarries, dressing and setting it – Caerfarchell, Pemb., 1827, had horse skulls laid into the stone foundations as it was said that this would kill the echo . . .

new chapels retained a loyalty to the ancient practice, though many chapels facades became flat surfaces which were painted according to a colour scheme defined by the architect.

In addition to those already mentioned, other good examples of the rural side-wall-facade chapels of this period might begin with Croes-y-parc, Peterston-super-Ely, Glam., Baptist, about 1780; the simple hipped-roof and ogee-windowed Capel Cae-bach, Llandrindod Wells, Rad., of 1804; the chapel-house of Horeb, Crai, Brec., Calvinistic Methodist, 1808 (25); Capel Cwm-bach, Carm., 1808; Woodstock, Pemb., 1808; the tiny Pennal, Glasbwll, Mont., Independent, 1822 (26, Plate 7); the dramatic Capel Adfa, Llanwyddelan, Mont., Calvinistic Methodist, *c.* 1820, with a black-and-white half-timbered extension to the side (27); the asymmetric Saron, Ty'n-y-rhyd, nr. Dolanog, Mont., Wesleyan Methodist, 1827; the wide complex of Jerusalem, Gwynfe, Carm., Independent, 1827; the extremely remote Soar y

24 . . . while the little Ainon chapel at Llanuwchllyn, Mer., has walls that are made of rough boulders graduated in size from the ground to roof.

25 Although town chapels of the early nineteenth century adopt the gable-end facade pattern, rural chapels were much slower to change. The chapel-and-house Horeb, Crai, Brec., still looked like farm buildings when built in 1808.

Mynydd, near the Tregaron end of Llyn Brianne reservoir, Calvinistic Methodist, 1828 (which doubled as the local school until 1947) (28); the red-brick Protestant Chapel, Llanfyllin, Monts, Independent, 1829 (built at government expense to replace a chapel demolished by a mob); Carmel, near Nantmel, Rad., Independent, 1829 (29); tiny Sardis, Cwmcamlais, Brec., Congregational, 1835 (30); the slated facade of Bethesda, South Dairy, Pemb., Baptist, 1832 (31); the crisp and wonderfully-sited Hawen, Card., Congregational, 1838 (Plate 9); tall-windowed Blaenannerch, Card., 1838 (the chapel of Evan Roberts, instigator of the 1905 national revival, whose spectacular conversion experience took place in the first pew to the left of the pulpit) (132); Bethel, Cynghordy, Denbs., 1840, at a rural crossroads, with a small house, and a letterbox and long bench built into the walls; Philadelphia, Nant-y-caws, Carm., Independent, 1841; strong-featured Brynberian, Pemb., Independent, 1843; Hen Gapel, Tre'r-ddôl, Card., Methodist, 1844 (32); Rhydygwyn, Felinfach, Card., Unitarian, 1848 (33); the legendary Salem, Llanbedr, Mer., Baptist, 1850, a powerfully-expressed asymmetrical facade, a fine raked-floor interior, the setting of Curnow Vosper's famous painting of the steeple-hatted and beshawled 'Welsh lady' (34); Bethel, Llangors, Brec., Calvinistic Methodist, 1852 (35); the fine complex of buildings that comprise Peniel, Pant-teg, Carm.,

26   27

The minute Pennal, 1822, at Glasbwll, Mont., was part of a row of farm buildings and distinguishable from them only because of its whitewashed facade (26). Capel Adfa is a large side wall chapel at Llanwyddelan, 1820, with a typical Montgomeryshire black-and-white half-timbered schoolroom (27).

28   29

The extremely remote Soar y Mynydd chapel in the mountains near Tregaron, 1828, a very long two-storey side wall design, was also used as the local school until the 1940s (28). Fine proportions and an elegant sense of scale dignify Carmel, 1829, near Nantmel, Rad. (29)

30 Assymetrical Sardis, Cwmcamlais, Brec., 1835, declares its identity as a church with its pointed windows.

31 Bethesda, South Dairy, Pemb., slated not only the roof but the whole of the facade and side walls in 1832.

32   33

The fine side wall-facade chapel of 1844 at Tre'r-ddôl, Card., has been converted into a museum (32). Rhydygwyn at Felin-fach, Card., 1848, integrates chapel and house (33) . . .

Independent, 1856; Hermon, nr. Llanfachraeth, Mer., 1865; Zion, Begelly, Pemb., 1866 (36); Nanternis, Ffynnon Dewi, Carm., 1867, with 'lamb-and-flag' window-glass; and Cwmsarn-ddu, Llandovery, 1857, with its open-air baptismal pond in a field opposite the chapel (125).

Examples of bigger two-storey side wall and square-plan chapels in towns would include the simple Caersalem, Dowlais, Glam., 1821; the fine Bethlehem Green, Neath, Glam., Calvinistic Methodist, 1828 (37); Zoar, also Neath, 1828, Independent, with a remarkable and unique plaque that contains a drawing of the chapel itself; Salem, Llandovery, Carm., Independent, 1829 (20); York Place, Swansea, Glam., Baptist, 1830, with a later porch; Capel y Cymer, Porth, Glam., 1834; Salem, Aberdare, Glam., 1841; Libanus, Pontypridd, Glam., 1841/46; the restored black-and-white Classic Carmel, Cefncoedycymer, Glam., Baptist, 1844; Gwernllwyn, Dowlais, Glam., Congregational, 1851, by William and John Gabe; Nebo, Hirwaun, Glam., Independent, 1851; and the chapel, schoolroom and chapel-house group, with puzzle-monkey tree, at Cadlys, Aberdare, Glam., 1866, seamlessly joined to the old Cadlys Arms, a thriving tavern even in the temperance hey-days of the chapel (38).

Capel Beili-du, Pentre-bach, Brec., Calvinistic Methodist, 1820, is perhaps the most classic example of the old rural traditions, a side-wall facade chapel, with tall round-headed windows, a tiny schoolroom and chapel-house – a building that nestles into the landscape and is at one with the nearby whitewashed farmhouses (Plate 8).

34   **35**

. . . as do the famous Salem, Llanbedr, Mer., 1850 (34), Bethel, Llangors, 1852 (35), and the unusual design of Zion, Begelly, Pemb., 1866, with the chapel, schoolroom, and chapel-house decreasing in size with a step-down roofline from left to right (36).

36

37

Two examples of large town chapels with side-wall facades and attached houses. Land prices shot up in the towns of industrializing Wales and gable-end facade chapels consumed less ground, but Bethlehem Green, Neath, 1828 (37), and Capel y Gadlys, Aberdare, 1866, used wide street-front plots to advantage (38).

38

CHAPTER 6

The Mid-nineteenth Century: Counting the Flock

From the middle of the century onwards most Welsh people lived their lives within the orbit of, or in relation to, the chapels. Their literacy, their world outlook, increasingly their politics, were deeply affected by the morality of the chapel, its often crabbed narrowness and its often sweeping spiritual vision, its populism, in both its warmth and deacon-controlled and often mean-spirited tyranny, its social equality, its opening to talent, particularly in verse and music, its whole style and manner, fragmented by Dissent's sectarianism and made porous by multiple variants and departures from Calvinism. . . . They came to think of themselves as classless, a gwerin *(folk) to use the popular term . . . and they were the real Welsh. As they became more radical in their politics they came to feel that they, as a Nonconformist people, were the Welsh nation. The Prime Minister, Gladstone, echoed this: 'The Nonconformists of Wales* are *the people of Wales.'*

Gwyn A. Williams, When Was Wales?, *Penguin Books, 1985*

The chapels were changing, but Wales was changing even faster: at breakneck speed industrialization and a growing population raced into the nineteenth century together. The impact of industrialization on the south of Wales throughout the century was massive and enduring. In 1800 some 20 per cent of the population of Wales lived in the two southern counties of Glamorganshire and Monmouthshire, but by 1900 some 65 per cent of the entire population was resident in the same two counties, and the population of Glamorganshire trebled in the period from 1850 to 1900. Cardiff, the capital city, was smaller than the iron-town of Merthyr, which was a world-leading exporter of metal goods. In a mining valley like the Rhondda, the whole population in 1850 had been about 12,000 but rocketed to 130,000 by 1900, and as coalmining became the major industry the workforce grew exponentially: in 1850 there had been about 11,000 miners in the whole South Wales coalfield; fifty years later there were over 200,000 of them. In 1800 some 80 per cent of the Welsh population lived in the rural areas; by 1900 80 per cent of it was in the southern towns. The chapel-building impetus moved with them and became a town-oriented activity.

The Nonconformist growth in the same period is a reflection of how it was to become the dominant non-industrial force. It gripped the public with waves of revival, led by imaginative, powerful and entertaining orators, in clean and tidy buildings that became, as we have seen, the religious, social, educational and musical and entertainment centres of each community. In the chaos of such rapid change and the overwhelming social pressures it generated, the chapel was one of only two after-work experiences available to most of the population – the other was the tavern. The chapel was a quiet sanctuary away from the filth of the mines or the noisy chorus of hammer and blast-furnace, filled with calm confidence and like-thinking folk, who rejoiced and sang in fellowship. Some historians have also mused on the probability that association with 'chapel' and everything it stood for in its broadest sense of friendship, responsibility, and sobriety, may well have been the opiate that helped calm a potentially explosive insurrection – although there were many risings and riots, they never developed into an all-consuming national revolution. Nonconformity moved from a minority position of despised Dissent to a central role, and would never return to the periphery of Welsh life. It had become a rock in the flood of change.

Out of the jumbled mass of social movement, several dominant forces can be quite well-identified. Firstly, there was the economic impact of the vast industrial revolution that was flaying the landscape of the south. Secondly, there was a revival of interest in the idea of a Welsh culture, expressed in music, literature, and the Welsh language – though it did not yet embrace architecture or much visual art. Thirdly, the effect of the work of the Church and the Nonconformists in the area of education was taking hold. Fourthly, the religious revivals gave a cohesiveness to society as eventually three-quarters of the whole population were to become associated with a church or chapel. Fifthly, the population grew and that growth was not Welsh-bred or Welsh-led – a huge number of immigrants arrived from England and Ireland. The issue of the increase in the population and its effect cannot be over-emphasized, for it was to change the culture of Wales, and also directly affected Nonconformist ambitions in evangelizing and chapel-building. The population had grown to about 600,000 in 1800, and it then doubled by 1850, and by 1900 had shot up to over 2 million. Between 1800 and 1850 the number of chapels went from 1,300 to 3,800. They were opening at a rate of about one a week.

In any study of Wales and Nonconformity, or the building of the chapels, the 'hinge' decade from 1850 to 1860 is a critical period. At one end is the 1851 Religious Census, which attempted a comprehensive national effort to 'enumerate the faithful' (in spite of the Biblical warnings about the inadvisability of doing so), and at the other stands the 1859 revival that washed across Wales like a flood tide, upon which was launched a vast chapel-building enterprise by the Nonconformists, but which also bore good fruit for the Anglicans. The year 1851 also saw the Great Exhibition in London, an event that symbolized a confident and wealthy nation's encapsulation of the 'Spirit of the Age'.

The stated purpose of the Religious Census was to ascertain what provision there was for worship in Britain (i.e. how many churches and chapels, and how many seats), but it did not count the professed *adherents* to the various denominations, which would have been a far more significant accounting. The forms employed were confusing and open to misunderstanding, and they were only printed in English so that in rural Wales incomprehension added to other problems. When the Census was published the matter of provision for worship was swamped by bickering over the numbers of persons attending the church or chapel on the day of the Census, and what constituted membership of either. Harsh words of accusation and recrimination resulted. The Nonconformists were accused of a 'conspiracy on the part of the Dissenters to inflate the number of attendants'. The Nonconformists countered with claims that the Census had been taken in March, a notoriously bad month for weather in Wales (Census Sunday was in fact a day of solid rain and storms) and that the servant classes in Wales, who would normally have attended chapel, were ordered to remain at their duties by the gentry.

The forms allowed for comments to be made by those completing them, thus affording fascinating insights into the religious temper of the country. The Vicar of Nevern, Pemb., raised the old problems of the difficulty of the Church conducting its pastoral mission in far-flung parishes: 'The distant inhabitants of my parish would be leading the lives of heathens had not the Dissenters built chapels in different parts – of which there are six.' The minister of the Independent chapel at Pan-teg, Mon., concluded his 'comment' with 'God Save the Queen and No Popery'. But the most bitter commentaries came from the Anglican vicars, doubling as Returning Officers, who were scathing about the Census and the Welsh Dissenters, whom they accused of outright lying about the numbers attending chapels.

The most thunderous denunciation of the Dissenters came from the Vicar of Abergwili, Carmarthenshire, who accused them of outrageous shennanigans, and paints a picture of Nonconformists scuttling about from chapel to chapel in the pouring rain: 'No reliance whatever can be placed on the accuracy of the Nonconformists' returns . . . there has been wilful exaggeration of which I could give shameful specimens in dissenting localities. There was an unseemly and irreligious plan of persons leagued together to run from chapel to chapel for the special object of cramming them . . . the same person is made to represent three or four different persons, and in this manner the number of Dissenters has been multiplied' (Ieuan Gwynedd Jones, *The 1851 Religious Census: The Returns for Wales* (two volumes), Cardiff, University of Wales Press, 1976).

In spite of all the rancour, the Census was of enormous significance for it demonstrated – even allowing for some slight waywardness in the arithmetic – the dramatic growth in Nonconformists and in the number of their chapel buildings, and provided a first mid-century appraisal of the Nonconformist achievement and a contrast with the situation of the Church. The statistics showed that the Church had

39 Open-air full-immersion baptism ceremonies, like this one at New Tredegar in 1843, were spectacles which drew great crowds – 10,000 people came to one of them at Llandeilo.

grown by some 15 per cent, while the Nonconformists had expanded by over 50 per cent. By the mid-1850s the vast majority of the population of Wales was in some way directly associated with a chapel. There were seats enough in the chapels to accommodate 75 per cent of the entire population. In Monmouthshire it was said that 74 per cent of the entire community was attending regularly, and 65 per cent of Merthyr Tydfil's inhabitants were chapel-goers, with 6,123 children attending the Sunday Schools of 33 chapels. Morriston's chapels were so capacious they could seat 84 per cent of the entire population. As a base-line comparison for the development of chapel-building the 1851 Census is invaluable for it can be compared with the 1905 Royal Commission Census, which shows that, while there were 393 chapels in the county of Glamorgan in 1851, this had shot up to 1,200 by 1905.

As the industrialization of Wales continued apace the skills of the chapel-builders were called upon in the erection of 'large sheds' for various 'works', with the result that many colliery buildings bear a distinct resemblance to chapels. The symbolism of linking piety with industriousness was not lost on either the Nonconformists or the employers who encouraged the thrifty, sober and hardworking chapel-goers, and association with a chapel could actually mean the opportunity for advancement at work. The Taff Vale Railway company stated in its 1856 Rule Book for employees that: 'It is urgently requested of every person on Sundays and Holy Days that he attend a place of worship, as it will be the means of promotion when vacancies occur.' As these hardworking men advanced themselves in this way, they became a major force in their community. It was said that the height of personal success was symbolized not only by the seat of authority in their work, but by a place in the Big Seat of the chapel, and that from this there rose an influential figure in Welsh industrial Nonconformity, the colliery manager who was a deacon in his chapel.

The Nonconformists in the hinge decade 1850–60 were a new breed, part of the mainstream of Welsh life, not reviled Dissenters who were excluded from it, and were still succeeding in attracting converts, aided by the revivals. The 1859 national religious revival was the real spur to chapel-building, and in the period from 1860 onwards some senior Nonconformists became so alarmed that it was branded 'a mania'. The Baptists, for example, had 230 chapels in Wales in 1830, which rose to 567 in 1860, and on to 742 in 1880, and to 896 in 1902. A valuation of the chapels assessed them at £340,000, while they collectively carried a debt of £85,000. Of these 225 were in Glamorgan and Monmouthshire. In the latter half of the century this denomination alone grew from membership of 40,000 in 1850 to over 100,000 by 1900. (Some 10,000 persons had attended one of their open-air baptismal ceremonies at Llandeilo, though their practice of ocean-baptism was scornfully dismissed as 'burial at sea'.) (39)

The Independents were to report in 1865 that they were opening chapels in England and Wales at a rate of four a week, had 'improved' over a hundred more to accommodate 60,000 new members, and planned to open 300 new chapels within three years at a cost of £95,000. The Welsh Calvinistic Methodists in 1895 accounted 2,794 chapels, over 145,000 members, and over 300,000 who came to listen, and that their collections for the year exceeded £300,000. Some denominational statistics showed that some sects had areas of extraordinary localized strength where they held sway – the island county of Anglesey became known as 'the Methodist chapel without a roof'.

CHAPTER 7

The Battle of Styles: The Classic and Gothic Revivals

CLASSICISM

From the 1840s 'building' falls firmly under the spell of 'architecture', and its magic becomes irresistible. As we have seen, until those years most chapels essentially were well-executed plans by gifted amateurs who articulated a quite limited vocabulary of design elements on the exterior, and adhered to a rigid Nonconformist format for worship and preaching in the interior. The inventiveness and sureness with which the chapel-builders marshalled the elements of a small kit-of-parts showed an extraordinary ability to create some delightful and robust buildings, usually with very limited means. But increasingly, the eye they had kept on the old traditions of Welsh building was distracted and dazzled by news from the east, from England, and the pages of the building journals of the day as they became more readily available to the chapel-builders. By the middle of the nineteenth century (and earlier in the towns of the south) the news of current 'foreign fashion' building practice was broadcast not only by journals, but also by the men of that practice, the trained professional architects. These were men who had no allegiance to the vernacular expressions of Welsh buildings: they were trained to propose and impose an entirely different architectural expression that was elevating, inspirational, in excellent taste, and was meant to 'improve' those who experienced it.

These architects were under a spell of an old enchantment, that of the ancient world. The lack of a common climate between wet Wales and sunny Greece, which would have made Classical architecture more appropriate, did not hinder their ambitions for a moment. They were absorbed with the models of the Greek and Roman architecture that had already had a huge impact in England before crossing the border into Wales. By the time it arrived it had been studied, interpreted, altered, applied, reinterpreted, amended, and handed on to others who would have their own opportunity to honour it, or mangle it. When the Welsh chapel-builders came under the spell of the Classic, they were not committed to upholding the purity of either the architectural expression or historical fidelity and accuracy.

1 The oldest surviving chapel in Wales, Maesyronnen, near Hay-on-Wye, converted from a barn in 1696, is largely original and untouched, a simple preaching-room with the intimate atmosphere and feeling of a well-scrubbed farmhouse kitchen.

2 The interior of Maesyronnen.

3 Capel Newydd is also 'a little granary of God' from the age of the 'barn-chapels' in the 1770s, on the Llŷn peninsula in North Wales.

The deep pews and high pulpits are characteristic of chapels of this period. The coffin-carrier hanging over the door was a powerful intimation of mortality and the focus of many sermons.

4

The remote and tiny Capel Beiliheulog, Gwenddwr, near Brecon, one of the first simple purpose-built chapels, which were usually constructed by the congregations contributing their own skills as builders, carpenters, tilers and stonemasons; it was built around 1740. The interior is equally simple, but the focus is firmly on the pulpit, as it is in every chapel. An early form of the elaborate later Victorian 'Big Seat' for deacons and elders lies below and in front of the pulpit, with a small table for communion.

5

6

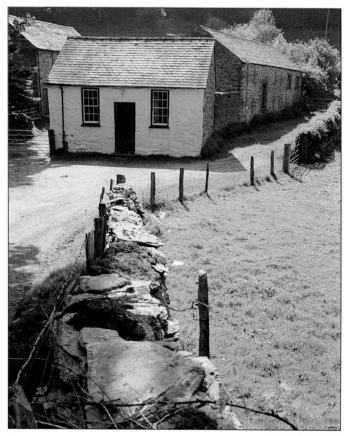

The spirit of Classical architecture appears in Welsh chapels in 1810 at Peniel, Tremadog (6), where a design based on Inigo Jones' church at Covent Garden, London, was the inspiration, and heralded the eventual breakaway from the vernacular Welsh traditions that had influenced the chapel-builders. The most significant aspect was the change from a facade on the side wall to the gable end, which would eventually dominate chapel architecture. Few congregations could afford a chapel as elegant as Peniel, and the minute Pennal chapel at Glasbwll is a stark contrast – it was built in 1822 (7).

7

8 The traditional vernacular architecture of Wales dominated the design of the chapels in the early nineteenth century – they looked like large barns, with the facade on the long side wall. Capel Beili-du, Pentre-bach, Brec., was built around 1820, with a little schoolroom and stores as part of the building, and the minister's house adjoining.

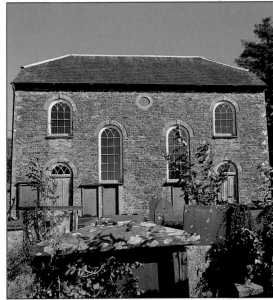

9   10

Hawen and the larger Llwynrhydowen, Card., chapels date from the 1840s and were designed to contain galleries to accommodate the rapidly-increasing congregations flocking to the chapels during the great religious revivals.

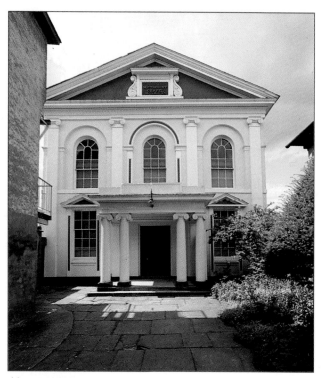

11

Most chapels in the early nineteenth century were designed by skilled amateurs – often the minister or a deacon – but when trained architects appeared the chapels began to look quite different: St James's Chapel in Monmouth, 1837, is a beautiful example of Classicism in both the facade and the fine interior. It stands in striking contrast to the earliest chapels like Beiliheulog, built about a hundred years before St James's.

12

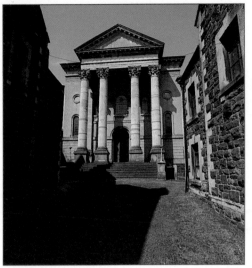

13   **14**

High Classic architecture in Carmarthen and Newtown, with dramatic and imposing facades featuring gigantic columns, used with great effect by the architect George Morgan in 1872 and 1881.

15   **16**

John Hartland was more restrained in his fine Tabernacl, Cardiff, in 1865, in contrast to the muscular 'two steps forward' facade of the Methodist chapel at Llanidloes by the Revd William Jones, who was one of a number of minister-architects who combined preaching with architecture.

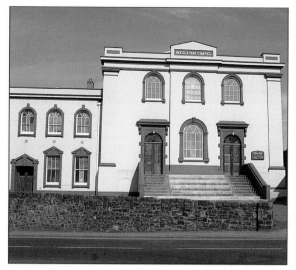

17

18

Congregations loyal to the long-wall facade often sliced off the old one and added a new, and expanded the building. The Wesleyan chapel at Haverfordwest also demonstrates a flat cement-render over the whole facade, which was then given a distinctive colour-scheme. John Hartland of Cardiff 'Classi-fied' the simple fieldstone facade of Capel y Carn at Bowstreet in a similar and highly effective manner in 1900.

19 The Cardiff architect and Member of Parliament, Sir Beddoe Rees, designed the Resolfen chapel that features one of his best interiors, with its graphic ceiling-beams, three-sided gallery, and recessed organ towering over the pulpit and Big Seat complex.

20 The influence of the British Arts and Crafts movement, the Beaux Arts of France and the Art Nouveau of Scotland began to appear in chapel architecture in the early years of the twentieth century. It penetrated to rural Llanarmon Dyffryn Ceiriog to shape this chapel in the very last phase of chapel-building, after the last religious revival of 1905.

21 Large and small, simple, majestic or merely pompous, the chapels of Wales are disappearing – at a rate of more than one a week. Dwindling congregations faced with the cost of maintaining costly buildings are being forced to leave them, and the ravages of weather and vandalism will lead to the demolition of temples like the decomposing Classical Glendower Street Chapel, Monmouth (21). Capel Mud on Anglesey is already gone, and no-one will will again 'Enter His Courts with Praise' at this abandoned Bethel (22, 23).

22

23

40   **41**

Athens comes to Wales. Classical architectural themes were employed by 'the new men' of
the chapels – the trained architects. Their introduction of themes from the history of
architecture severed the old ties with vernacular Welsh building traditions. Crane Street
chapel, Pontypool, by J.H. Langdon in 1847, has a powerful Classical temple portico, and
equally strong interior in the Greek 'cella' style (40, back cover). Caersalem, Caernarfon, was
a very early example of the second contestant in the Classic vs Gothic 'Battle of Styles', a
Gothic facade in 1826 (41). Beulah, nr. Margam, replays Lombardic themes in a very rare
round-plan chapel in 1838 (42), while the Baptist Temple, Newport, in 1843 (demolished), is
the simplest stereotypical Welsh chapel of the Classically-inspired period (43).

42   **43**

44   **45**

The materials used by the architects varied a great deal, sometimes directly affected by local
availability, but also improving transport systems meant the importation of more unusual
materials. Various kinds and colours of Welsh stone dominate – roughly-finished, hammer-
dressed or carefully cut, there was great pride of workmanship among the masons who built
the chapels. Cana, Felindre, 1857 (44), and Nolton Haven, 1858 (45), both in Pembrokeshire,
show fine masonrywork in smaller chapels . . .

Each architect was independently employed by each independent congregation,
and they all worked independently of each other (though prolific chapel-building
architectural practices would develop in due course). This is an important point for
each chapel is essentially an entity unto itself, and was never required to work with
any other, or be answerable to any higher authority (such as one that could guide the
architectural expression of chapels and apply norms or standards). As a result, the
very independence of the congregations as they commissioned architects to build for
them was a guarantee that there would never be a cohesive chapel style, or a national
school of Welsh chapel architecture. The chapels all have common characteristics, so
they are all the same – but every one is different. . . . They are the same and as
different as the congregations whose whims, opinions, taste, and budgets, caused the
chapels to be built.

The inevitable consequence of the appearance of the architect was that the
vernacular expression quickly fell away, and was replaced by the application of
the Classic. They could study the available earlier texts and portfolios of
reproductions of Classic forms like *The Antiquities of Athens* by Stuart and Revett

46

47

. . . Big town chapels were showcases for the craftsmen who relished an opportunity to show their skill with granite, limestone, Welsh Blue Pennant, and even imported marble: Bethel, Aberystwyth, 1888, by the minister-architect Revd William Jones (46), and two fine chapels by Owen Morris Roberts, Capel Coffa Emrys, Porthmadog, 1879 (demolished) (47), and his Moriah, Llangefni, 1897 (48), are excellent examples.

48

49   **50**

Brick became popular, initially around the kiln-town of Ruabon, and with the spread of a rail network it was employed by architects throughout Wales. The Welsh Baptist chapel at Denbigh used a soft-toned red brick for its gable-ended Georgian chapel in 1836 (49), as did the side-wall facade of Penarth, Llanfair Caereinion (50).

(which appeared from 1762 to 1788), giving the period of the Classic revival the title of 'The Folio Age'. There also appeared journals of the profession and the building world like *Building News* and *The Builder*, while the denominational magazines like the Independents' *Annibynwyr*, the Methodists' *Yr Eurgrawn Wesleyaidd* and *The Nonconformist* spread the news about chapel-building and the styles being adopted, which would influence the appearance of the chapels in Wales.

Peniel, Tremadog, as we have seen, was a delicate and fine example of the well-proportioned and thoughtful application of a Classical idiom to a Welsh chapel form – and was accepted by a willing congregation, who would never have seen its like. For a congregation to make the transition from a simple chapel redolent of a barn to a Greek temple, was quite a step. The Greek style had already had a revival in England from around 1805, but it was a style that lent itself most readily for application to civic architectural development rather than religious structures. It did not suit Anglican church-builders, the boxy 'cella' form of the Greek temple being quite unsuited to Anglican or Catholic forms of worship, but it was a form that was very appropriate for the Nonconformist chapels.

51   **52**

A fully-rendered cement veneer over the whole facade was a popular choice for architects who wanted to emphasize a flat overall treatment, sometimes with mouldings, strips, columns and window-surrounds painted in contrasting colour schemes. Fine Classical chapels like St James's, Monmouth, 1837 (Plates 11, 12), Bethesda, Rogerston, Mon., 1834 (51), Bryngwyn (52), Newcastle Emlyn, Carm., 1843, and the Wesleyan chapel, Haverfordwest, 1865, show this tendency . . .

If Peniel was a first toe-in-the-water, then the Pontypool Baptists had full-immersion Classicism in 1845. Crane Street Chapel, Pontypool, Mon. (40, back cover), was designed by J.H. Langdon, and built at cost of £2,200, with a dramatic and dominating street presence – a Greek revival portico of grand scale, muscling up to very small and narrow courtyard. The congregation established a building fund in 1839, and by 1845 had enough to buy a slim freehold plot in the town centre, and commission Langdon to erect the chapel. When it opened in April 1847 the chapel had collected £1,000 in subscriptions toward the cost, but like many congregations they elected to carry a debt and reduce it over time by enthusiastic fund-raising – it took this particular congregation 21 years to clear their burden of £1,200.

Although the Greek revival had faded away in England by about 1840, Crane Street Chapel is a confident and powerful statement of undiluted Athenian revivalism, a bold status-symbol facade probably based on a direct Classical reference (the gateway of the Acropolis in Athens), but also probably by way of the Euston Railway Station archway of 1837, in London, one of the most celebrated engineering and architectural wonders of the Victorian Age, or, closer to home, the Ionic style of the Royal Institute at Swansea (now the Swansea Museum) of 1840, and the Doric Town Hall of Bridgend, 1842, by Frederick Long and David

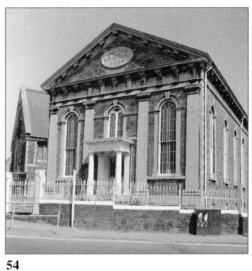

53   **54**

. . . while three Llanelli chapels, Siloah (53), Greenfield (54) and Bethel (55), also employ it to accentuate their Classical references . . .

55

Vaughan respectively, or the Greek revival County Hall, Brecon, 1842, by Wyatt and Brandon.

Architectural revivalism and the 'Battle of Styles' between Classic and Gothic held sway in England as it was to in Wales, and the architectural plagiarists borrowed freely from the histories of style and pasted their favourites on to the chapel facades. There is one specific revival style, however, that never appeared in any form on any Welsh chapel: the Egyptian. An Egyptian architectural revival had occurred in England, but had faded away by the time the Welsh chapel architects were coming into their own. The Welsh congregations were avid readers of the Scripture and were especially fond of the Old Testament, and their view of the Egyptians was of a demonically evil force – to emulate their architecture would have been unthinkable. Interestingly, the congregations found the Classic expression, associated with the pagan Greeks and the martyring Romans, to be initially more acceptable than Gothic, which was associated with the Anglican Church, and was largely favoured by the Wesleyan Methodists.

As the religious revivals affected the congregations within the chapels, so architectural revivalism would affect the outside. The two-storey gable-end facade begins to dominate chapel design from the 1830s, and becomes the overwhelmingly accepted form by the 1850s. The speed of the transition from the old vernacular traditions is most obvious, unsurprisingly, in the southern and industrial townships. It provided 'the new men', the architects, with an essentially blank canvas on which to create a new tradition of chapel architecture. It did not take long. The work of most chapel architects between the 1840s and the mid-1850s was rooted in Classicism, but its essential character was that they expressed it with a light touch. The acceptance of these restrained designs signalled that they were popular with congregations and endlessly replicated. It is not until the 1870s and 1880s that we find an enthusiastic Greco-Roman architect from Carmarthen, George Morgan (1834–1915), who would usher in unrestrained High Classic chapel architecture (Plates 13, 14).

The Battle of Styles in England, which pitted proponents of the Classic against those of the Gothic, was also fought in Wales; the winner was the Classic, but it was on points rather than a knockout. However, the architects who were practising in Wales in the 1830s to the 1870s were raising hundreds of chapels that as yet had very little reflection of the Gothic revival – Caersalem, Caernarfon, Baptist, 1826, is a very early and rare exception (41). The character of the chapels of the mid-century is that of a modest Classic expression, a sureness in handling the proportions, and the ability to combine the best materials in inventive and pleasing ways. Although constrained by the obvious limitations of the gable-end facade, which is little more than a square with a triangle on the top, these architects engage in a series of themes-and-variations that seem endless. At one end of the spectrum were scholarly exercises that were intended to look at home in Athens, and at the other the whims of local builders.

The latter must mostly account for the odd-man-out octagonal chapel, the survivor of the very few Welsh 'round chapels', Beulah, Groes, nr. Margam, Glam., Calvinistic

56   57

. . . It is particularly successful on Classical chapels, and very effectively used by the architects of Glendower Street, Monmouth, 1844 (abandoned) (56, Plate 21); Zion, Carmarthen, 1850 (57); Tabor, Pentrefelin, 1860 (demolished) (58); Ynys-gau, Merthyr Tydfil, 1853 (demolished) (59) . . .

58   59

60

61

. . . Llan-non, Card., 1865; Siloam, Bethesda, Caern., 1872 . . .

Methodist, 1838, reputedly by C.R.M. Talbot of Margam Abbey, at a cost of £800 (42). He gave the land and promised to provide the materials cheaply, on the condition that the chapel was built to his own design. It was said to have been inspired by an octagonal building on the Continent, and he wished to see one on his own estate at Margam. If this is so, the obvious references to Wesley's fondness for octagons may be discounted – though Beulah *is* a Methodist chapel – but a local historian reported that Talbot's inspiration did not come from the Lombardic or 'Continental' styles he had seen in Europe, but from the design of the Chapter House at Margam.

By the 1850s the two-storey gable-end facade, no matter what application of style lay upon it, had settled to a widely-accepted format. The gable-end was characterized by the careful disposition of, usually, three windows in the upper facade, and two in the lower, flanking the door, and a declaration of identity by name and denomination on a plaque, often in the centre of the triangular pediment. The Baptist Temple, Newport, Mon., 1843 (43), serves as a typical Classically-influenced chapel of this type. Architects would make play with all these elements, especially the central window, but the format as seen had become somewhat standardized, though there are extraordinary variations within the stereotypical facade.

The surface treatment of the facade of the chapels of this period is usually expressed in a flat rendering, with low relief details, or in lightly-textured surfaces of worked fieldstone. A fine example of this, a particularly stern Classicism with lightening Doric touches, is Seion, Twynyrodyn, Merthyr, Glam., 1841. Also, Cana, Felindre, Pemb., Independent, 1857 (44); Nolton Haven, Pemb., Independent, 1858 (45). Later examples

62   63
. . . the Roman basilica of Tabernacle, Haverfordwest, 1874, by Lawrence & Goodman; and
Bethel, Llanfor, Mer., in 1880.

of exceptional quality include the Calvinistic Methodist chapel at Llandeilo, Carm., 1874; Wesleyan chapel, Llanidloes, Mont., 1874 (by Richard Owen); Bethel, Aberystwyth, Card., Baptist, 1888 (by Revd William Jones) (46); Capel Coffa Emrys, Porthmadog, Independent, 1879, for £5,120 (demolished) (47), and Moriah, Llangefni, Ang., Calvinistic Methodist, 1897 (48) (both by Owen Morris Roberts) for £5,500.

The traditions of loosely-coursed dressed stone and random-rubble disappeared, and the appearance of well-dressed masonry in Pennant stone began to gain great popularity, its subtle colour variations much appreciated, but the danger of its dourness usually being relieved by coloured trim in a contrasting sandstone, or occasionally brick. Brick was used for the entire fabric of a chapel in areas nearer the brick factories centred on Ruabon before it became popular in the rest of Wales. The Welsh Baptist chapel at Denbigh, 1836 (49), is a fine early town example, as is the more rural side-wall-facade Penarth chapel, Llanfair Caereinion, Mon., c. 1830 (50).

Fully-rendered cement veneer surfaces became common, which served to emphasize that flatness of the overall design which is then accented by a few carefully-introduced ornamental elements as counterpoints, like columned porches, painted mouldings and window-surrounds. Examples include the early and beautifully-executed St James's Chapel, Wesleyan Methodist, Monmouth (Plates 11, 12), and Pont-rhyd-yr-ynn, nr. Cwmbrân, Baptist, both in Monmouthshire in 1837;

64 John Hartland of Cardiff built a number of well-designed chapels in a crisply-delineated Classical style, with his Tabernacl, The Hayes, Cardiff, in 1865, being the boldest of them, the main facade with two arcades of doors and windows flanked by projecting staircase bays.

the Baptist chapel at Rogerston, Mon., 1835 (51); rural Bryngwyn, Newcastle Emlyn, Carm., 1843 (52); the Wesleyan chapel at Haverfordwest, Pemb., 1865 (abandoned) (Plate 17); Siloah, Independent, 1840 (with twin porches in 1853) (53), Bethel, Baptist, 1850 (55), and Greenfield chapel, Baptist, 1858 (54), all three in Llanelli, Carm., bearing a distinct stylistic relationship. Also, Glendower Street Chapel, Monmouth, Congregational, 1844 (abandoned) (56, Plate 21); Zion, Carmarthen, Presbyterian, 1850 (57); Tabor, Pentrefelin, Caern., 1826 and 1860 (demolished) (58); Ynys-gau, Merthyr Tydfil, Glam., Independent, 1853 (demolished); Llan-non, Card., Calvinistic Methodist, 1865 (60); Siloam, Bethesda, Caern., Presbyterian, 1872 (61); while a Roman basilica landed in Pembrokeshire in the form of

65   **66**

Classical architecture provided inspiration both general and specific. Two popular motifs used by many chapel architects were the Palladian triple-window, and the 'halo arch'. The first is seen at Ivor Street Chapel, Dowlais, 1860 (65), and Capel Y Graig, Newcastle Emlyn, 1878 (66), which derive from the sixteenth-century Italian architecture of Palladio. In Wales it became known as the Trinity window . . .

Tabernacle, Haverfordwest, by Lawrence and Goodman in 1874 (62); and finally the thrusting Bethel, Llanfor, Mer., *c.* 1880 (63).

Perhaps the best of these is Tabernacl, Cardiff (popularly known as 'Tabernacl, The Hayes'), Baptist, 1865 (64, Plate 15), by John Hartland, built in a record six months, with a wide facade with two projecting bays (to carry the stairs to the gallery), four entrance double-doors with large round-headed windows directly above, each with elaborate stained-glass: all-in-all one of the finest chapels and most original of the period.

The central upper window of the facade became subject to a quote from Venetian architecture with the appearance of the triple window, the centre one large and rounded, flanked by two smaller ones. This device is often also known as a Palladian window (being based on the architecture of sixteenth-century Italy and the work of Palladio that was popularized in Britain by Inigo Jones) and Ivor Street Chapel, Dowlais, Glam., Congregational, 1860, by John Gabe, is a good representative of this type (65), also Capel Y Graig, Newcastle Emlyn, Carm., Baptist, 1878 (66). In Wales, however, the Palladian window became known as a Trinity window, and as a consequence it virtually never appears in this form on Unitarian chapels. The Italian Renaissance also contributed an arch that began to appear on the chapel facades from about 1855, sometimes assertively breaking through the lower pediment moulding; it was probably

67

68

. . . The 'halo arch' is based on the church of San Andrea, Mantua, Italy, by Alberti, and was popularized by the minister-architect Revd Thomas Thomas, who applied it to his own chapel at Landore (68), and to Bethania, Bethesda (69), and Salem, Porthmadog, 1860 (67).

69

70   **71**

Ebenezer, Swansea, 1868, combines both the Trinity window and the halo arch (70), which is to be seen at Llanuwchllyn (71), while Llangloffan spreads its across the whole width of its facade (72), and a geometric double-chevron version appears at Mount Pleasant, Holyhead, in 1885 (73).

72   **73**

74   75

The High Classic style appeared in chapel architecture from the 1860s, sometimes in a more restrained form – the Wesleyan chapel at Carmarthen, 1860 (74) – but more robustly at Penmachno, 1873 (75), and the large Argyle chapel, Swansea, 1873 (76).

76

77   **78**

Dramatic High Classic chapels by a master of the style, George Morgan of Carmarthen –
Lammas Street Chapel, Carmarthen, 1872 (Plate 13), Mount Pleasant, Swansea, 1874
(77, Plate 14), and Newtown Baptist chapel, Mont., 1881 (78).

introduced and popularized by the minister/architect Revd Thomas Thomas 'Glandŵr',
and was based on the church of San Andrea at Mantua, Italy, by Alberti. It became
sentimentally known in Welsh chapel architecture as the halo arch. Salem, Porthmadog,
Caern., Independent, 1860, by Thomas, is an early example (67). Thomas' own chapel,
Siloh Newydd, Landore, was designed by him with Thomas Freeman, a deacon, using
the arch in a dramatic manner (68), repeated in the red-brick Bethania, Bethesda, Caern.,
1885 (69); Ebenezer, Swansea, Glam., Baptist, 1868, combines both the halo arch and
the Trinity window in one facade (70); also the historic Llanuwchllyn chapel, Mer.,
Independent, 1870 (71); the Baptist chapel at Llangloffan, Pemb., 1862 (72), with the
halo arch stretched across the whole facade; and a curious geometric variation with an
inverted 'double chevron', Mount Pleasant, Holyhead, Ang. (73).

A more overt High Classic style developed from the 1860s, expressed by architects
with a greater sense of confidence and drama, which led to chapels that are grander
and clearer in their commitment to replaying ancient models. In the county town of
Carmarthen, the Wesleyan Methodist chapel, 1861, is an elegant Ionic-columned
temple (74), while the rural hamlet of Penmachno, Caern., can be proud of Bethania,
1873, in the modified Welsh Corinthian style contrasting dressed sandstone with
rugged fieldstone walls (75). A smoother surface, painted, was used for the huge
recessed portico in the Composite-Doric style for Argyle Street chapel, Swansea,
Glam., Presbyterian, 1873, by Alfred Bucknall (76).

A trio of especially exuberant High Classic expressions are by the great chapel
architect George Morgan (of Carmarthen, with a practice eventually taken over by

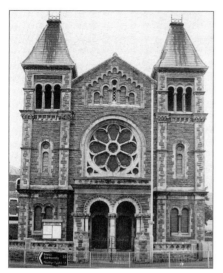

79

80

George Morgan's Lombardic and Romanesque 'themes and variations', with distinctive wheel-windows, for the Baptists at Frogmore Street, Abergavenny, 1877 (79); Bethesda, Haverfordwest, 1878 (80); Ebenezer, Port Talbot, 1880 (81); and Dinas Noddfa, Morriston, 1884 (82).

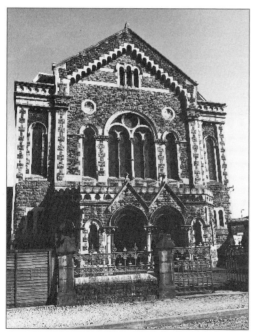

81

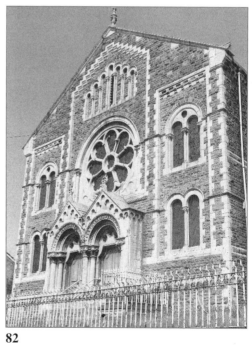

82

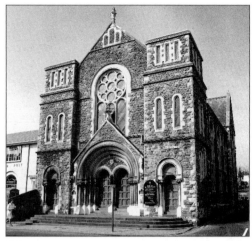

83   **84**

Architects employed Classical elements but were not sticklers for historical accuracy or purity. They mingled styles and periods, but mixed in features that they found appealing, or just invented them, and many chapels are 'collages' of motifs and themes rather than facsimiles of ancient models. Bethesda, Swansea, 1870, mixes Doric and Corinthian themes, with added mini-turrets of unknown origin. Mumbles chapel, Oystermouth, 1877, is Romanesque by way of Morgan of Carmarthen . . .

his son, Howard Morgan), vast and dramatic High Classic chapels like his Lammas Street Chapel, Carmarthen, 1872 (Plate 13), Mount Pleasant, Swansea, 1874 (77, Plate 14) and Newtown chapel, Mont., 1881, for £8,000 (78), all of them for the Baptists. His later work shuffled Lombardic and Romanesque elements in strong-limned facades – examples of his 'theme-and-variations' approach are the four muscular Baptist chapels at Frogmore Street, Abergavenny, Mon., 1877, for £4,200 (79); Bethesda, Haverfordwest, Pemb., 1878, for £2,199 (80); Ebenezer, Port Talbot, Glam., 1880 (81); and Dinas Noddfa, Morriston, Glam., 1884, for £3,500 (82).

Other powerful High Classic expressions include: Bethesda, Swansea, Glam., Baptist, 1870, a dramatic facade mixing Doric and Corinthian themes, a half-round projecting porch, and four columned mini-turrets perching on each corner of the roof (due for demolition) (83); Mumbles chapel, Oystermouth, Glam., Methodist, 1877, by A. Totten for £3,500, in a style highly derivative of George Morgan (84); St Paul's, Aberystwyth, Methodist, 1879 (85); Capel Coffa Eglwysbach, Pontypridd, Glam., Wesleyan Methodist, 1899, in red brick with blond Corinthian sandstone pillars (converted to a community health centre) (86); the robust Romanesque of Capel Salem, Senghennydd, Glam., by the Revd William Jones (abandoned), with its dramatic doorway (87, 88); Peniel, Amlwch Port, Ang., Presbyterian, 1900 (89); and Y Tabernacl, Llandudno, Caern., 1901, by G.A. Humphries (90).

85 86

. . . while St Paul's, Aberystwyth, 1879 (abandoned), is a less adulterated Classicism. Capel
Coffa Eglwysbach, Pontypridd, 1899, counterpoints un-Classical red brick with sun-bleached
sandstone Corinthian columns.

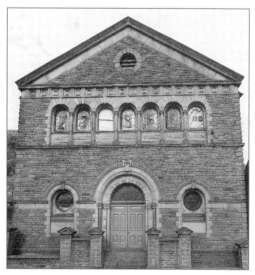
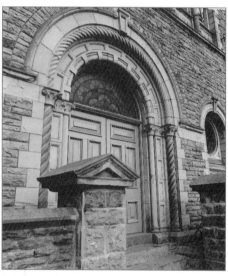

87 88

The Revd William Jones employs a robust and confident variation of the Romanesque with
arcaded windows in his Salem, Senghennydd, 1899 (abandoned).

89

Peniel, Amlwch Port, Ang., in 1900 and Y Tabernacl at Llandudno, 1901, are late variations of moderate and high Classical interpretations.

90

91

92

'The Cathedral of Welsh Nonconformity', the largest, grandest and most expensive chapel built in Wales: Tabernacl, Morriston, by the architect and deacon John Humphrey in 1872, at the breathtaking cost of £18,000. A rare photograph shows Tabernacl covered in huge timber scaffolding as construction reached the base of the tower and spire.

93

94

95

The fame of Tabernacl spread throughout Wales, and Humphrey was invited to repeat the success of his design – though no other congregation could raise the money to duplicate the tower and spire, or the lavish interior. Three variations of the original Tabernacl were built: the Llanelli version of 1873 had the same name (94), then came Zoar, Swansea (95), and Zion, Llanidloes, 1878 (96), all of them for the Congregationalists.

96

TABERNACL, MORRISTON

The chapel which is generally considered to be ultimate evocation of all that a chapel could be is known as the 'Cathedral of Welsh Nonconformity': Tabernacl, Morriston, Glam., Congregational, 1872 (91, front cover). The architect was John Humphrey of Mynyddbach, a deacon in Tabernacl. The cost was a staggering £18,000. The chapel completely dominates Morriston by dint of its size and thrusting steeple, and its placement on the brow of a sweeping hillside, allowing for a huge schoolroom to be built into the foundations. The design was the result of the triumvirate of the minister (William Emlyn Jones), the architect (Humphrey), and the contractor (Daniel Edwards) entering into a compact to erect the grandest chapel ever seen in Wales. They succeeded. *The Cambrian* newspaper stated in an editorial in January 1873 that 'Tabernacl stands out as one great redeeming feature in the whole of that manufacturing district, an oasis in a desert, an object worthy of admiration in the midst of unsightly works and manufactories of every size and description. It will amply repay a visit, even if made on foot over the worse roads in the Kingdom, and all who have seen it speak of it in the highest terms.'

The minister and the architect went from Morriston on a tour of Britain, looking at the newest and best of the Nonconformist chapels, before returning and creating a design which was Classical in inspiration, Lombardic in tone, and was a collage of the elements they liked best. There are eight huge Corinthian columns, linked by arches, and a steepled tower with its unusual octagonal spire. Although the emphasis is on the facade, the three other sides are all fully designed. The interior is the equal of the scale and quality of the facade, with a gallery that goes around all four walls, carrying the organ and the choir seating behind the pulpit, dramatically swooping down behind the pulpit/Big Seat complex. Few chapels were recorded by the camera during their erection, but Tabernacl, photographed swaddled in massive timber scaffolding, is a rare exception (92).

The chapel was widely reported and John Humphrey was asked by other ambitious congregations if he could create reflections of Tabernacl in other new chapels – though none could afford to duplicate the steeple (93). Humphrey obliged them with further Tabernacls, at Llanelli, 1872–3 (94), Zoar, Swansea, at a cost of £2,400 (demolished) (95), and Zion, Llanidloes, Mont., 1878, for £1,550 (96), all of them for the Congregationalists. In terms of sheer grandeur Tabernacl is probably matched only by George Morgan's enormous Baptist church at Newtown, Mont., of 1881 (78).

These examples by Humphrey and Morgan essentially show a basic set of components being masterfully juggled by a good architect, to produce very similar buildings, but each with a strong architectural personality of its own.

THE GOTHIC REVIVAL

The emphatic inspiration of Greece and Rome became leavened with the appearance of chapels whose design derived from the Gothic, which began to gain increasing influence after about 1860. The English debates over what was the appropriate style for church and chapel architecture were known in Wales, in part from the increasing number of English architects called to execute buildings in the Principality, but also from the very public debate of the issue in the magazine *The Ecclesiologist*, on whose pages the architectural combatants at Oxford and Cambridge aired their views with regularity, Oxford championing the Gothic pointed arch as the most seemly style for Christian worship, while the Cambridge men encouraged study of church design from the Middle Ages. The effect of these encouragements was felt more acutely in England, where they were put into practice, but the Welsh Nonconformists tended to accept stylistic change more slowly, and the Nonconformists' buildings of this period retained some characteristic Puritan simplicity.

The Gothic was favoured in Wales after 1860, especially by the English-speaking Wesleyan Methodists, while the Welsh-speaking congregations retained a distrust of the Anglicans' pointed arch. Where the Gothic was used it appears in a rather debased form, and certainly few architects who built in this style were rigid adherents to the purity of expression recommended by *The Ecclesiologist*. Even so, the appearance of the Gothic was a sign that the chapel architects were moving their interest from the Classical world and the Italian Renaissance, to the architectural forms of medieval France, Holland, Germany, and the Gothic cathedrals. There was a view expressed that Classicism was staid and dull, while Gothic was dynamic and inspiring. *The Ecclesiologist* magazine had come to the conclusion that the Classical style had too strong a whiff of pagan pantheism, and recommended good Christian Gothic.

The finest example of the Gothic in Wales (with French overtones) was executed at Pembroke Terrace, Cardiff (now converted to an architect's offices) (97), for the Calvinistic Methodists, in 1877, by the architect Henry C. Harris, who later built another fine Gothic work, St David's, Pontypridd, Glam., Presbyterian, 1883 (98). Other examples include the Presbyterian chapel at Llandinam, Mont., 1872, by Szlumper & Ardwinkle, for £1,720 (99); George Morgan's North Road Baptist chapel, Milford Haven, Pemb., 1878, for £2,427 (100); Bethany, Baptist, 1882, by E.A. Johnson, in red brick with creamy sandstone dressing (101), and Whitefield chapel, Presbyterian, 1907, probably by Beddoe Rees with tower and a dwarf spire (102), both in Abergavenny, Mon.; Castle Square Presbyterian chapel, Caernarfon, 1879, by Richard Owen (103); Trinity Methodist, Cardiff, 1897, by A.V. Ingall (104).

The most exotic of these Gothic chapels is at Charles Street, Cardiff, Congregational, 1855, by R.G. Thomas, who created a building that could easily be taken for a Anglican church. The exoticism comes from the stonework on the facade – the architect is said to have written to every head of state in the world to obtain a lump of native stone from each, to cement into the facade of his new chapel as a symbol of God's dominion over the earth: the front of the chapel is 'a lesson in theology and geology' (105).

97 The finest Gothic revival chapel in Wales, by Henry C. Harris, built in 1877 in Cardiff, shown in a perspective illustration by the architect.

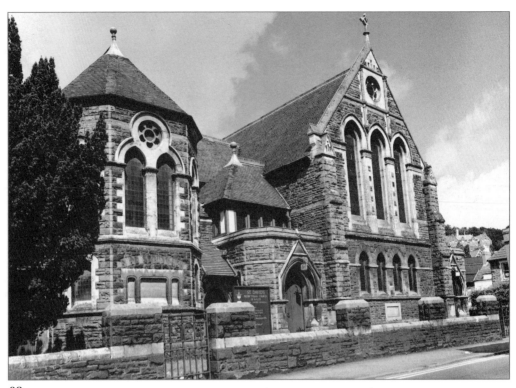

98

Though he died a young man, Harris built other chapels: his St David's at Pontypridd, also a
Gothic expression, was constructed in 1883 (98). Gothic was not as popular as Classical
styles – many Welsh congregations associated it too closely with Anglican churches and
shied away from it. Architects nevertheless found English-language congregations less
worried by that association: Szlumper & Ardwinkle built a Gothic chapel at Llandinam (99),
the ever-versatile George Morgan designed North Road Chapel in Milford Haven (100) . . .

99

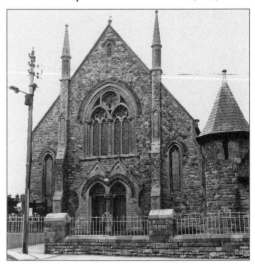

100

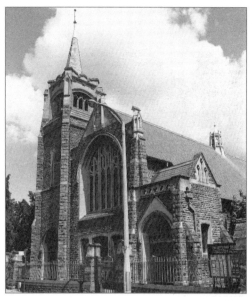

101

102

. . . E.A. Johnson built Bethany, Abergavenny, in red brick and blond sandstone in 1882
(101), and Beddoe Rees designed the Whitefield chapel in the same town in 1902 (102). The
Caernarfon chapel by Richard Owen, chapel-builder extraordinary, dominated the town
square and competed with the castle for attention (103), and at the other end of the country,
Trinity Methodist, Cardiff, featured a true spire (104).

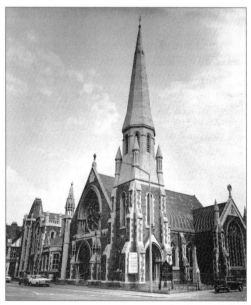

103

104

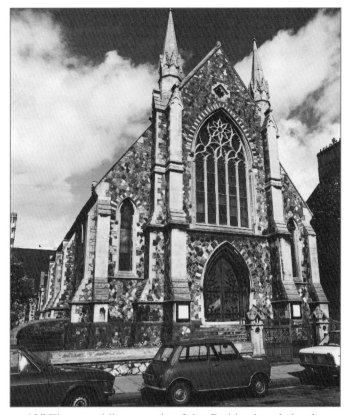

105 The most idiosyncratic of the Gothic chapels by the
architect R.G. Thomas, on Charles Street, Cardiff, could
easily have been mistaken for an Anglican church when he
built it in 1855. He incorporated a stone 'from every nation'
as a symbol of God's universal power – the facade was a
lesson in theology by way of geology.

As the towns of the south began to expand, land prices went up. The costs of
building followed, and congregations tried to keep these down by continuing to lend
their skills to the construction work, but it was easier to do this in the countryside. In
the towns the purchase of land on which to erect the new Bethel or Bethesda put the
Nonconformist denominations in competition with market forces, and sometimes in
rivalry with each other for the acquisition of a site. This situation affected the design
of chapels. Few congregations could afford to buy or long-lease the wider street-
frontage needed to build a traditional side-wall facade chapel, and the slimmer gable-
end facade design slipped into the narrower, deeper and cheaper building plots. Thus
the gable-end chapel with its emphasis on the bright-faced facade became the most
rapidly-adopted form in the towns, on confined sites.

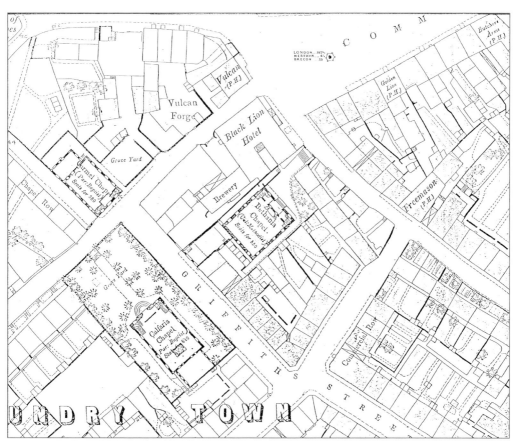

106 A map of the Foundry Town area of Aberdare in 1868, shows the sites of three chapels, the brewery, and a number of pubs. Bethania is shown tucked away on a land-locked site behind a row of houses and reached by a narrow lane – a fate that befell some congregations who bought these less expensive plots of town land. Some chapel architects like George Morgan in Carmarthen (Plate 13) and that of the St James's Chapel, Monmouth (Plates 11, 12), turned such problems to advantage and used the slim forecourts to focus the eye on the powerful chapel facade they created as an eye-stopper.

A map of the Foundry Town area of Aberdare, in 1868, shows the plots of land occupied by chapels (106). The largest, for Calfaria Baptist chapel ('seats for 840') was an expensive investment for the congregation – it was a substantial corner site, with a large graveyard at the front and space for a vestry or schoolroom at the rear. Almost opposite is Carmel, also Baptist ('seats for 380'), again with a graveyard, paralleling 'Chapel Row', and to the east across Griffiths Street is Bethania, Calvinistic Methodist ('seats for 550'). The plan clearly shows Bethania on a trapped

107 While some chapels leapt out at the passer-by, others like Upper Boat, Pontypridd, were part of the continuous strip of terraced houses and modestly blended in with them.

site, tucked well back and behind other houses, and reached by a gap in the strip of houses and front-gardens: Bethania lay uncomfortably close to the Black Lion's brewery – and within 500 yards of these three chapels were six other taverns. Bryn Sion, Dowlais, and Adulam, Merthyr, and the aptly-named Narrow Chapel, Rhyl (with no side windows), are other examples of chapels tucked away on awkward, unglamorous but less expensive plots of land. Some chapels were not on discrete plots at all – the chapel at Upper Boat, Pontypridd, is part of a long continuous terrace of workers' houses typical of the coalmining valleys, its facade flush with theirs, but with a tiny forecourt to dignify the temple (107).

CHAPTER 8

From Building to Architecture: Toiling for Temples

The spate of chapel-building in South Wales during the age of faith and prosperity which spanned the last century (and the beginning of this), gave us many atrocities in architecture, but there are a few good examples of what design can be under the master hand . . . the styles were bastards, begotten of an unholy union between pseudo-Classic and a depraved Perpendicular style, and sometimes a fake Decorated influence crept in slyly to upset any balance that might have been achieved.

Michael Llewellyn, The Sand in the Glass, *John Murray, 1943*

Until about 1840 there is virtually no reference to anyone acting as a chapel architect, and it is extremely rare for the word to have been applied to anyone associated with chapel-building – it is applied retrospectively by chapel historians but almost never in the contemporary documents. As a result very little is known with any degree of specificity about the men who created the early purpose-built chapels, or what formal background in building they may have had – if any. Although they created the buildings, they are the anonymous 'forgotten men' of the Welsh chapels.

Until the beginning of the 1850s chapel-building had been largely in the hands of 'planning preachers, designing deacons and contracting congregations'. The minister or a deacon would draw up a simple plan and elevation, and the congregation would pitch in with whatever specialist skills they could contribute to execute the plan. From about 1850 this tradition gradually fell away, though as we shall see, there are many instances of direct labour contributed by the congregation throughout the century. For example, it took the Baptist congregation at Sutton, Pemb., two years to build their Bethel, and they recorded the activity:

The brethren had been meeting in cottages in 1836 . . . but the Revd David Davies of the

Haverfordwest Baptist College arranged the exchange of a piece of land in the town for one at Sutton, which he then gave to the them on which to build a chapel. Our modern practice is first to engage an architect to draw up plans and specifications, and then invite tenders for the work . . . but at Sutton we bought materials directly from John Jardine, Haverfordwest, the builder's merchants, beginning on June 7th. 1837 and continuing to May 1839. The various purchases included pitch-pine, deal, mamel deal, white lead, linseed oil, hearth laths, dry hair, sprigs, spikes and paint. The materials were bought and the work done by the men, paid on a day-by-day basis, until the building was finished.

The men of the congregation were often skilled in an applicable craft – stonemasons, roof-tilers, carpenters, etc. – and a very large percentage of the chapels built in the first half of the nineteenth century had some direct physical contribution to the building by these men. As the century progressed the congregations employed professional architects whose technical specifications for the chapel, complete with more demanding architectural treatment, usually meant that the congregation entered into a formal contract with a builder to erect the chapel for an agreed price. The congregation would then turn its attention from lending their hands in labour to inventive fund-raising skills, engineering events to get money for the chapel-building fund.

The building of a chapel was a prodigiously expensive undertaking, but the congregations willingly took this on, saddling themselves with debt that could take decades to repay. The congregations themselves were the principal funds-givers or fund-raisers, though it was common for ministers to go off collecting on preaching-tours – even as far as London – to plead for funds for the new chapel. The minister at Struet chapel, Ystrywaid, actually went from door-to-door begging for contributions. The ministers themselves were far from well-paid, and they almost all had other employment. In the late eighteenth and early nineteenth century they were primarily craftsmen or they farmed in some small way, but by the middle of the nineteenth century shopkeeping was the predominant second occupation, followed by schoolteaching. In the 1860s the average salary for a minister in the south was about £60 per annum, and many of them were struggling to stay above the poverty level. Many congregations could hardly pay their minister, and got into serious difficulties in times of recession when they fell short of income to repay a building loan. (It is worth noting that at the height of the chapel-building boom there had been three pay-cuts of between 30 and 60 per cent for workers in Merthyr Tydfil – and these were the very people who were fuelling the frenzy for new chapels – while in 1872 and 1875 the coalminers' wages declined by 25 per cent.) The Baptists developed the Case Committee to help chapel-building congregations by assembling a list of potential contributors and acted as a referral agency. Eventually they created The Baptist Building Fund in 1824, and over the following twenty years it assisted sixty Welsh congregations. There was an ulterior motive at work in the case of the Baptist

Union and its Fund, for they were becoming increasing worried that in spite of revivals, too many chapels were being built and the denominational organizations experienced a nagging worry about the local rivalries and 'competition for pew-fodder'.

They were very careful as to where they loaned their Building Fund monies, in an effort to have some measure of control – their concerns were justified as the chapel-building mania eventually led to an enormous uncleared national debt. The other denominations also had similar agencies and Building Funds, with that of the Wesleyan Methodists being exceptionally well-organized and administered, with a building advice office that could recommend architects to aspiring congregations. At their 1855 meeting in Llanrhaeadr the Methodists' Chapel Loan Fund for North Wales met to disburse £3,000 to congregations who had plaintively written for help, mostly 'to relieve the heavy debts that press us so wearily and hinder our efforts to extend the work of God'.

Very few congregations – if any – were themselves rich enough to fund the building of a new chapel unaided, so they resorted to various means of gathering funds. Apart from the obvious (borrowing from a bank or one of the denominational chapel loan funds), they organized *Cymanfaoedd Canu* (the great singing festivals that became the places where classical music and oratorios were first performed in Wales), poetry readings, *eisteddfodau*, bazaars, children's crusades, and 'lantern lectures' (one of these, a very popular four-hour illustrated history of the Crimean war, raised over £1,000 for a new temple). The inevitable gigantic tea-party (*te-parti mawr*) was a popular attraction with 700 attending in 1862 to help Nebo chapel at Pen-rhys Mountain, with the record being set in 1853 when 2,113 sat for tea at Aberdare. In 1857 when the 100 women members of Jerusalem, Rhymni, had succeeded in collecting £100 each they symbolically burned the debt notes in a ceremony at the chapel. Contributions were sought from the great, the good, and the rich – asking someone to sponsor the laying of the foundation stone was popular. Preaching festivals that featured 'kings of the pulpit' were common: the High Street Baptists at Merthyr Tydfil took collections totalling £902 at the opening day 'preach-athon' in 1900. The powerful and immensely popular hymn 'Cwm Rhondda' ('Guide me O thy Great Jehovah'), was first performed at Capel Rhondda, and the rights sold to generate funds for the chapel.

Notoriously, a kind of lottery was invented, called The Art Union, which succeeded in raising the huge sum of £884 for Tabernacl, Merthyr, in 1866. Soar, Ystalyfera, offered a prize of £100 and a harmonium valued at a further £24. A Dowlais chapel was threatened with prosecution from the civil authorities for 'gambling', for these Art Unions were little more than chapel-sponsored betting: they lost all credibility after the lottery to aid a chapel at Maerdy, in which the deacons won all the prizes.

Congregations who had accepted the weight of debt to build anew kept a sharp eye

108 When congregations could not afford a complete rebuild, the reworking of the facade was an alternative, and adding convenient weatherproof porches was a popular treatment. The old side-wall facade of Capel Mawr, Denbigh, had a large box-porch added in 1829 . . .

on the chapel as it rose, perhaps put on their guard against the evil forces described in 1822 by the Anglesey preacher John Elias:

Be watchful against the devices and inroads of Satan in the erection of chapels . . . the Great Enemy endeavors to bring in confusion and so injure the good work. . . . Satan is not pleased to see Christ enlarging His Tabernacle. Satan will endeavour to hurt the cause in some way or another. . . . Wherefore, brother, be sober and watch unto prayer. . . . In all meetings with respect to the chapel let your conversations be quiet, kind, and guarded. Pray much for the Lord's countenance on the work otherwise the new chapel will answer very little purpose. O, abide with us, blessed Lord, or we shall see many of our large and excellent chapels empty.

John Elias, in Thomas Rees, History of Protestant Nonconformity in Wales, *John Snow, 1883*

The rural congregations, in particular, saw themselves as simply getting on with building a chapel as practically and as inexpensively as possible, with the idea of being part of a changing 'style' far from their minds. The modest secretary of Zoar, Llan-teg, in 1854, described an odd unanticipated problem that arose from the amateur design of their chapel:

> Architecturally – if such a grand word may be permitted – the little sanctuary of Zoar is of rather peculiar shape and form. From about the middle of the floor space in the direction of the pine-end, opposite the pulpit and the Big Seat, all the seats are on an inclined plane, forming what is called a 'rising gallery'. This implies a certain amount of space beneath, and at one time a small door led to this from the kitchen of the chapel-house, which was the caretaker's cottage. The original object of this was to provide room for that functionaries [*sic*] coal and firewood . . . but one old sister who fulfilled that office added to the usefulness of this 'crypt', by keeping a number of chickens there, but because the male birds were apt to compete with the musical performances on the upper side of the beams and boards, it was closed up.

THE ARCHITECTS

There is a notable sense of reticence on the part of the chapels themselves to claim too much for these men or their buildings. Such humility and avoidance of show that might imply a reference to church architecture is especially characteristic of chapel records until about 1840. This is in accord with the modesty of the buildings themselves, for few congregations thought of their chapels in such grandiose terms as being 'works of architecture'. Chapel histories tend to avoid the use of the word 'architect' (which implies that the holder of that significant title has formal qualifications) until about 1850 when a sense of pride over the employment of a *pensaer* (architect) appears with regularity in the printed histories. These histories were usually produced for a centenary or jubilee celebration, and are the most useful and significant repository of the histories of the various chapels, packed with information and anecdotes. Before the middle of the nineteenth century the chapel historian (who was usually the incumbent secretary of the chapel, working from the minutes, the treasurer's ledger and the membership records) would report that the 'plans were drawn up' by a member of the congregation, or even the minister himself. Often there was no accurate record of quite which member of the congregation was the planner, but designing ministers are usually identified. (These printed histories are as frustrating as they are informative, for they usually contain, for example, the names of every organist the chapel has ever had, and the names of everyone who contributed to the building fund, and who was at the dedication ceremony – and what they ate at the tea-party – but regularly omit the name of the architect!) In spite of this tendency, however, the later nineteenth century chapel histories often record with a flourish the identity of the designer, and even refer to his other works as testimony to the wisdom of the congregation in employing such a respected architect.

109 . . . Pentŵr chapel at Fishguard had its 1824 facade rebuilt in 1899 with added porches . . .

110

As already noted, the congregations invariably contained men who were skilled as artisans in some aspect of the building trade, and contributed those skills in various ways, some even taking on the responsibility of the design or of the whole building project. Chapel historians tend to use the words 'builder' (e.g. 'Mr Jones, a deacon, built the chapel in 1834'), or 'designer' (e.g. 'Bethel was built in 1820 from a design by the Minister, who had been a joiner before he was Called'), or 'planner' (e.g. 'The plans for the Tabernacle were made by Mr Evans, one of the elders') and use them interchangeably, but they invariably mean a person with practical skills in building, but not the possessor of a qualification that read 'Architect'. The possession of such a qualification was fairly rare in Wales until after the 1850s, and the ultimate accolade of being accorded recognition by the national agency was rarer still (that agency, the Institute of British Architects, was founded in 1834, becoming the Royal Institute of British Architects in 1837, while the other major force in formal architectural education, the Architectural Association, was created in 1847).

Architects such as Richard Owen in Liverpool, and the other giants of chapel-building in North Wales, Richard Hughes and Richard Davies, both of Bangor, had dynamic architectural practices that specialized in chapels, and between them were responsible for several hundreds of chapels – Davies is often said to have over 250 to his credit. Practices like that of Habershon, Pite and Fawckner in Newport, Mon., designed many chapels in South Wales, as did the Gabes of Merthyr, Beddoe Rees in Cardiff, Evan Griffiths of Aberdare, and the legendary George Morgan of Carmarthen (later with his son Howard Morgan), who was the architect for twenty-eight school boards, built the School of Art in Carmarthen, and dozens of chapels for the Baptists. R.G. Thomas of Newport built a handful of extraordinary chapels before emigrating to become the Government Architect in Australia. The North Wales architect Owen Morris Roberts was a ship's carpenter who trained himself to become an architect, and built a number of substantial well-designed chapels in the north. In the case of the architect Henry C. Harris, who died at the age of 34, he left fewer than five buildings, but his Gothic chapel in Cardiff is one of the finest in Wales.

Most chapels were, however, created by architects who may have built no more than two examples, and who therefore did not either develop a distinctive style or have opportunities for their work to mature. The independence of each congregation gave them the choice of going to a well-regarded chapel-building practice, or staying closer to home and employing a local talent (though some were not very talented), almost invariably at a saving on architects' fees. Each congregation contracted with the architect to design and oversee the building of the chapel, and each independent congregation was responsible for raising both the chapel and the funds for it. It was natural for them to employ architects who had built chapels for their denomination elsewhere, and thus came recommended, and it was a discernible trend that congregations would favour architects who were members of a chapel of the same denomination as themselves. George Morgan of Carmarthen, for example, was a staunch Baptist and was exclusively commissioned by them to build new chapels. This exclusivity and denominational favouritism was a contributory reason to the rareness of open architectural competition for chapels in Wales, though the practice was common in England. Siloh, Aberystwyth, was awarded a prize of £5 in open competition for a new chapel in 1859.

To erect a building the size of a chapel, a twentieth-century architect would draw up a lengthy list of specifications, accompanied by much cross-checking and reference to building regulations, the advice of the quantity-surveyor, engineer, etc., and draw up many pages of plans detailing the design. The Victorian architect, in contrast, often supplied as few as two drawings (a plan and an elevation – though these were even sometimes combined into a single drawing), accompanied by a written specification, which was, *de facto*, the contract. A competent and experienced builder, however, would be readily able to complete the whole chapel from this lean provision. What was not included in the plan was discussed on-site in detail as the structure rose from its foundations. The architect was contracted to create both the specifications and the drawings, and to oversee the works (see Appendix One for a detailed example of an architect's specification for a new chapel, and Appendix Two for the detailed cost-breakdown of building a chapel).

It may seem surprising that so few of the plans of the thousands of chapels drawn up by architects have survived, but it appears that they were largely unique drawings – the Victorian architect did not have the modern convenience of a plan-photocopier to turn out numerous prints. The plans were usually drawn up on a robust material like a canvas-backed heavy cartridge paper, or on linen, and were then handed over to the contractor who kept the plan on-site, where it suffered considerable wear-and-tear as it was consulted, usually to the point of virtual destruction by the time the building was finished, at which point it was discarded.

Some congregations perhaps just could not face the idea of the debt they would incur in building anew, or their building was adequate but tired and simply needed a sprucing up. Many architects were engaged to graft on a status-symbol in the form of new facade, joined on to the old chapel, for this is where all attention was now focused. Often in the case of an entirely new chapel the costs for the rest of the structure were reduced in order to give the best treatment to the 'shining face'. This was not lost on a wag who observed:

> The Trellwyn Methodists have built a church
> The front looks like an abbey,
> But thinking they can fool the Lord
> They've built the back part shabby.
>
> *Michael Llewellyn*, The Sand in the Glass, *John Murray, 1943*

Examples of the reworking of a facade, or the addition of new porches, are: Capel Mawr, Denbigh, Presbyterian, 1829 with a large new porch added by Edward Peters

111

. . . and Capel y Carn, Bowstreet, had a whole new facade added to the 1833 chapel-and-house by John Hartland in 1900 (also Plate 18).

112

in 1880 (108); Siloah, Llanelli, Carm., Independent, built in 1840 but with large twin porches and bridging canopy added 1853 (53); Hen Dŷ Cwrdd, Merthyr Tydfil, Glam., Unitarian, the 1853 facade replaced 1895; Pentŵr, Fishguard, Pemb. (109, 110), Calvinistic Methodist, the 1824 facade rebuilt with porches in 1889; Capel y Carn, Bowstreet, Card., Methodist, the 1833 building designed by William Jones for £502, completely reworked by John Hartland in 1900 (111, 112, Plate 18); Blaenau Gwent, Abertillery, Mon., Baptist, 1906, by N. Gasenius Lewis, for £4,867, grey Gothic confectionery (113).

The 'grafting-on' technique was popular among many congregations, but most were intent on building a new chapel, a much grander course of action that would inevitably focus attention on them. Perhaps the most interesting and clearly-demonstrated example of 'having it both ways' is Capel Caeo, Carm., Calvinistic Methodist, built as a side-wall facade chapel parallel to the road in 1837; in 1907 the chapel was renovated and the entrance doors on the side wall were made into windows, with the facade switched to the gable end (114).

Some chapels chose to rebuild and avoid any accusation of 'facade-ism' or being a 'shabby abbey' by treating all four sides of the building, an excellent example being Rhydwilym, Pemb., Baptist (immersion ceremonies in the river that runs along the edge of the chapel ground), built 1875 with slated side wall (115). The Baptist chapel Bethabara, built two years earlier at nearby Pontyglazier (116), has an identical facade layout to Rhydwilym, with a cement render, and the same anonymous designer may have built both – though in the latter he omitted the idiosyncratic low-relief clock painted on to the upper facade, its hands permanently indicating the eleventh hour.

There is no question but that there was a tremendous amount of inter-denominational rivalry going on, and some serious one-upmanship was at work: chapels at Pwllheli and at Llanrhyddlad, Ang., were consciously built with spires as jibes to the local Anglican churches. During the building of a new chapel a congregation was displaced, and had to find other accommodation, and turned to nearby chapels of the same denomination to help as friendly neighbours. There is a persistent legend that the congregation of Noddfa, Treorci, continued to worship in their chapel while the new Noddfa was built around and over the old one, which was then demolished and carried out through the front doors of the new chapel! (Documentary evidence to support this wonderful story has not appeared.)

Nonconformist congregations were essentially democratic in nature, so a majority vote by the congregation was required before the planning for a chapel could begin; some congregations were not convinced by their ministers or deaconate that a new building should be built or could be afforded, and they could vote the proposals down or register strong disapproval. For example, a third of the congregation of one of the grandest chapels in North Wales, Siloh, Llandudno (117), voted against the new chapel plan in 1899, though it was eventually erected by G.A. Humphries, an agent of the Mostyn Estate, who also designed nearby Y Tabernacl (90). Some ministers refused to abide by the vote of the congregation and the design of the new Wesley chapel at Merthyr Tydfil in 1866 was due to a unilateral decision by the Revd Josiah Matthews (118):

> He was most energetic and zealous in the building of the chapel. The site was fixed, but there was a difference of opinion about the size – he wanted a large chapel, the others a smaller one and they refused to yield. The site was marked out with stakes and everyone went home. Josiah Matthews waited until night and crept down to the field, pulled up the stakes and moved them further back, filling in the old holes so as to leave no trace. He went home secure in the gratification that he had done a good thing. He was not discovered, building began, and the secret of the shrewd brother assured the gain of this subtle matter, and the beautiful and commodious chapel we now see.
>
> History of the Wesley Chapel, *Merthyr, 1966*

Each chapel was a unique building as each congregation was, in essence, a law unto itself, and its taste and budget would determine what it would build. This could lead to difficulties, whether an architect was employed or not. In 1824 the congregation of Ebenezer, Newport, employed two deacons who were carpenters to build a new chapel, and the cost of £1,800 was said to have made it one of the most expensive built in Wales. They had received 3*s* 6*d* per day for labour and supervision, and were reimbursed for the materials needed, to create a building that was to last 73 years without alteration – but the congregation stripped them of their membership for having been so profligate, and loading an unwelcome debt on to the membership.

In 1862 the congregation of Hermon, Bridgend, eventually refused to employ an architect because the professional fee of £27 was too great a burden to bear, and they designed it themselves. At Tal-y-bont, Card., the architect-builder in 1855 failed to complete the work for the agreed sum and the congregation had to turn to a skilled deacon to finish the chapel.

By the mid-century, however, there was a very rapid decline in the number of buildings being designed by any member of a congregation, and it became standard practice for them to engage an architect proper to design the new chapel. Not all of these were local architects, or even Welsh, for architects from Bristol, Derby, Birmingham, Liverpool and London were employed to build chapels for expanding congregations, though there were plenty of local designers to call upon. Of these, a notable group comprised the reverends who combined very successful preaching ministries with equally successful practices as chapel architects. Most, though not all, designed chapels exclusively for their own denominations. At Landore, Swansea, the dominant figure was the Revd Thomas Thomas, known as 'Glandŵr', whose chapels were built in a style described by *The Builder* magazine as 'Landore

113 Blaenau Gwent sliced off the front of its chapel and had a vast neo-Gothic nose added by N. Gasenius Lewis in 1906.

Lombardic' (Bethania, Bethesda, Caern., 1885, in red brick (69)). The Revds Evan Harries of Merthyr (described as 'that old amuser Harries, had been a carpenter by craft, who favoured a squared plan for his chapels saying that they were easier to preach in, and gave good oratorical space'), Joshua Watkins of Llanwenarth and Carmarthen, Thomas Morris (known as 'Ten Chapel Tom'), William Jones of Ton Pentre, David Jenkins and Thomas Morris of Llandeilo, E. Roberts, William Humphries of Swansea, William Davies and his son Revd Aaron Davies of Rhymni, William Jones (who is said to have designed over two hundred chapels) and his son-in-law architect W.D. Morgan, and William Edwards of Caerphilly, were all both noted preachers and architects (Edwards achieving renown as a builder of bridges, barns, houses, foundries and mills, and as the town planner of Morriston).

These were well-informed and educated men who had far more than a smattering of understanding of architectural history and form, and who in all probability had

114 From side-wall facade to gable-end facade in the same building. Capel Caeo was a side-wall facade chapel when built in 1837, but was modernized in 1907 when the side wall doors became windows, and a gable end entrance became the dominant feature.

access to useful contemporary texts which commented on the current trends in chapel-building, both in Wales and in the rest of Britain: *The Builder* and *Building News* are representative examples. Much of the practical aspect of the elements that went to make a chapel were to be found in the readily-available builders' books of the period, which were catalogues of the component parts of buildings that could be ordered and delivered. Gone were the days of the hand-built chapel springing from the contiguous landscape, with every element crafted in the skilled hands of the congregation – now stone, brick, iron railings and gates, and even elaborate plasterwork was imported for the new Bethels.

Some congregations still played a practical role in the erection of the new chapel even though a contractor might be undertaking most of the building. In 1804 the congregation at Llangrannog noted that 'few of us could give money, but we all helped to find materials and to build the chapel. Some worked the stone, some did the hauling, some gave beams or slates or wood.' Such activity was characteristic of the earlier period, but it was still in practice a hundred years later, when Ebenezer, Abertillery, was extended: 'The digging of the foundations was done by the members of the chapel in 1877, and they dug them again when we built a schoolroom in 1904.' In Prestatyn in 1825 'The faithful and hardworking men of the congregation blistered their hands night after night toiling in the quarry after completing a day's work, to gather stone for the chapel', while in Abertillery in 1854 'they toiled feverishly and persistently to make their dream into a temple'. Ministers took care of matters spiritual and physical: 'The Reverend Jones worked along side the other men, overseeing the work, and carrying stones and the like', in Pontlotyn, 1877.

Congregations who built their own chapels usually did so over an extended period, and had to wait for funds or materials to become available before proceeding with the work. Many chapels built in this piecemeal way suffered damage from winter storms and rain during extended periods of construction – the Ebbw Vale Baptists had a roofless chapel, and a gale eventually blew down the walls. The Wesleyan chapel at Swansea was both large and roofless (visitors thought it was Swansea Castle) and remained so for four years until it opened, as a historian subtly stated, 'with the stimulating challenge of a huge debt'. The costs of building chapels at Aberafan in 1821, Hirwaun in 1837 and Sirhowy in 1847 were so great that the congregations had no money for pews and sat on simple benches. The Wesleyan chapel at Caernarfon in 1826 was said to be the largest in Wales, and had cost a breathtaking £4,000 – thirty years later the debt had only been reduced by £500. At Hengoed in 1831 the Baptists took down the old chapel and the best timber was recycled to become the pulpit and Big Seat of the new. It took the congregation at Capel Newydd, Lampeter, three years to complete their chapel, while at the other end of the spectrum the new Wesleyan chapel at Sketty, by the architect Alfred Totten in 1875, was completed in two months.

There were conferences and gatherings where news of chapel-building was exchanged, and annual publications like the nationally-distributed *Congregational Year Book* commented on trends in chapel design; the 1847 issue was especially significant as its leading article and editorial were about chapel architecture, in marked contrast to the lack of concern about such matters evidenced by earlier denominations. Even more surprising is that the Editor, after reviewing a history of chapel-building, determined that there had only been two architectural forms:

. . . both of which were associated with two potent systems of false religion; the Grecian architecture identified with the temples of Minerva and Jupiter and all the abominable idolatries of a classical mythology; and the Gothic or pointed architecture adopted to the shrines, high altars, sacristies and Lady chapels of Popish superstition.

Having warned his readers of the danger of infection from these styles, he went on to dismiss the barn-chapel tradition, and even the preaching-houses of John Wesley, before reluctantly allowing that a few Nonconformist chapels already built in the Classic style may have some merit. But the most astonishing aspect of the Editor's recommendations is his statement that the design of the building was paramount, and his criticism of chapel-builders when he thought that 'architectural proprieties are being sacrificed . . . to seeing and hearing'. Should there be a misunderstanding about his position, he restated it: 'If an edifice is to possess any architectural pretensions whatsoever, the requirements of sight and sound must not be rigidly enforced.' The absolute belief of previous Nonconformists was that the building was simply a house for a pulpit, and that everyone in that house must be able to see and hear the occupant of that pulpit, with everything else secondary to core belief. But the Editor of the *Congregational Year Book* laid his emphasis on adherence to architectural style and taste, even at the expense of a good view of the preacher, a very different attitude of mind from that which we have seen guiding the building of chapels. He encouraged congregations to pay close attention to the architectural style of their new chapel as they had 'no need to build a barn-like place of worship. When money is to be spent for the service of God, we are bound to use it with taste and judgement, so as to attract, rather than repel persons of intelligence and respectability.' Finally, required to make a recommendation as to quite what style is favoured for new chapels, after reviewing eleven newly-built temples (one was 'Roman', one was 'Grecian', one was 'Italian', three had no style but were 'commodious', and five were adaptations of the 'Gothic'), the Editor came down on the side of the pointed arch and advanced the Gothic cause.

If congregations were influenced by such commentaries, and many were, they must have concluded that they would need a great deal more information and expertise than had been available in the past to build their simple chapels. The new chapels were to be more in style and abreast of fashion, and an architect was therefore essential to guide the congregation in achieving it. This is a critical point for it signals the willingness of the congregation to accept the disruptive influence of an architect – disruptive in that he brought to new chapels an architectural style that was alien to Wales and, more than disrupting the continuum of chapel-building design that was linked to the barn-chapel vernacular expression, he severed it completely.

There were some useful preparatory guides in the form of books (though these were all in English) that could provide a measure of inspiration, provide models

115

116

Rhydwilym chapel, 1875 (115), is a duplicate facade of Bethabara at nearby Pontyglazier, the first in dressed stone, the second in unifying cement render – but note Pontyglazier's permanent 'Eleventh-hour' clock painted on to the upper facade as a reminder to passing sinners that time was running out (116).

117 One of the grandest of the North Wales coastal chapels, the massive red sandstone of Siloh, Llandudno, by G.A. Humphries in 1899, with huge twin stone cupolas.

of form and plan, and give practical advice about legal issues, contracts, and how to negotiate with an architect. The earliest of these appeared in 1820, the comprehensively but ponderously titled *Observations on the Fitting-up of Meetinghouses for Public Worship, illustrated by Plans, Sections and Descriptions – including one lately built in the City of York, embracing particularly the Method of Warming and Ventilating*, by William Alexander. This was followed by volumes as various as Gilbert Scott's *Domestic and Secular Architecture* (1858), which was a licence for wholesale borrowings from the history of architecture, Cubbitt's very practical advice in his 1870 *Church Design for Congregations*, F.J. Jobson's *Chapel and School Architecture* (1850). Ronald

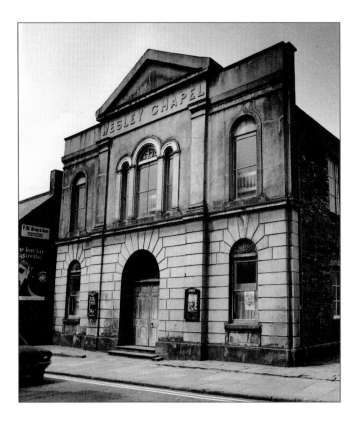

118 Wesley chapel, Merthyr Tydfil, 1866, is bigger than intended – the minister crept to the site at night and moved the builder's markers to increase its size. The facade at street frontage is like an impressive stage-set, and demolition of adjoining buildings reveals that the sides were never intended to be seen.

P. Jones's *Nonconformist Church Architecture* was published in 1914, far too late to be useful.

Only one book by a Welsh chapel architect appeared, largely as an advertisement for his own practice, and illustrated with examples of chapels he had already built or proposed to build: *Chapel Building – Hints and Suggestions*, by Beddoe Rees, of Cardiff. (He was Sir Beddoe Rees, MP for a Bristol constituency. He was a leading Nonconformist, who was denied permission to marry in the chapel at the House of Commons for that very reason, with attendant public outcry and extensive newspaper comment). By the date of its publication in 1905, Wales was caught up in the excitement of the final religious revival and the last spurt of chapel-building before the onslaught of the First World War, by which time chapel-building had virtually come to a complete halt.

On Christmas Eve 1891, the greatest Welsh chapel architect of them all died at his home in Liverpool, and a few days later over six hundred people came to pay their respects by attending his funeral. Richard Owen (born 1831) was a hugely successful architect, the most prolific chapel-builder in Wales, and a self-made man. He was born at Four Crosses, Caern., became a skilled carpenter and joiner, went to Liverpool when in his twenties, joined a company of surveyors and estate agents, and

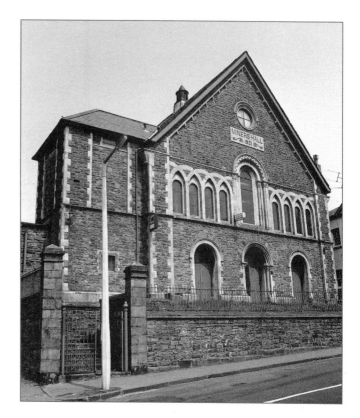

119 A mystery chapel. The Miners' Hall, Merthyr Tydfil, was originally a chapel, built at the expense of the Taff Vale Railway to replace a chapel it bought and demolished for the site of its new station. Legend has it that this new chapel was designed on the spot by the company's engineer, the great Isambard Kingdom Brunel, in 1853.

attended night classes in building and architecture. He founded his own architectural practice at the age of 30 in 1861 and began as he was to conclude, by building a chapel – for the Welsh Presbyterians in Everton. This was the first of many that Owen (and later his son, Hugh Owen) was to build all over Wales, though the practice was based in Liverpool, where he designed domestic and civic buildings and was a comprehensive town-planner. As he built so his fame as a designer of well-proportioned and economic chapels increased and he was asked by many congregations, especially in North Wales, to design their new temples. His skills were so respected that he was known not simply as an architect, but as the leader of his profession – in Wales he was called the 'arch-architect'.

By the time of his death Richard Owen was the designer of at least two hundred chapels, though there is enough circumstantial evidence to believe the obituarist who wrote that 'it had been computed that he drew up the plans for some three hundred places of worship in the Principality'. However, when he died his skills – and those of the other chapel architects – were being called upon less frequently as chapel-building, once 'a mania', was slowing down, and the magnetism of the chapel was less powerful than in previous decades.

120 The once-modest Nonconformists were originally reluctant to trumpet their identity, but as the nineteenth century wore on their reticence disappeared and the names of their chapels were emblazoned across the facade, as here at Nazareth, Penrhyndeudraeth.

An odd footnote to chapel architecture in mid-century is the possibility that the legendary railway engineer Isambard Kingdom Brunel may have designed a Wesleyan chapel at Merthyr Tydfil (converted to other use, currently abandoned) (119). It is said to have been erected at the expense of his employer, the aforenoted Taff Vale Railway, in lieu of an older chapel that sat on the site Brunel defined for a new station. If true, then the Romanesque chapel with clever facade arcade of linked arches of 1853 is his only known work in Wales – though Trinity Methodist chapel at Risca, Monmouthshire, 1852, bears a distinct resemblance.

WALES AS THE HOLY LAND

Brunel's Merthyr chapel was converted to the Miners' Hall, and the large original plaque was removed. Plaques and annunciation-panels or strips appeared on the facades of chapels in a multitude of styles, shapes and typographical forms (120).

This 'naming' not only gave the basic information about name and denomination, but also served another purpose, which was to unite, in the minds of the congregation, their temple with those in the Scriptures: Wales became the Holy Land.

Most congregations, steeped in Bible study, chose to name their chapels after a location mentioned in the Bible, heavily favouring Old Testament place-names. As all vestiges of Nonconformist reticence disappeared, the chapels often placed large plaques on the facade to declare their identity (for example Nazareth, Penrhyndeudraeth, Caern.); many of these neatly fitted into the triangular pediment of the gable-end facade. They usually broadcast the name and the denomination, but often carried the date of the building. As the century wore on the plaques would tell the tale of successive rebuilds, improvements, extensions and refurbishments; some even recorded the name of the builder or the minister. Others carried simple salutations like 'Hosanna Alleluia', or, as in the case of the confrontational Unitarians of Ammanford, 'Vox Populi, Vox Dei', while the Unitarians of Cefncoedycymer, Merthyr, declared on their facade that 'There is but One God, the Father'.

In many a chapel Sunday School hung maps of the Holy Land with Wales drawn on top of them, uniting the Principality with the sites of historic religious events – thus Mount Ararat became Snowdon. If there was some way in which the name could relate to the part of Wales, or some feature of the landscape where the chapel was built, then they readily co-opted it and emphasized the association. The popular Libanus, for example, is the Welsh variation of Lebanon (a mountain range); Elim was a spring or well surrounded by large trees; Bethabara a ford in a stream; Bethcar the house of the Lamb of God; Carmel a garden in the mountains; Zion a fortified hill; Peniel a fertile place near a river; Siloam a pool connected with baptism and Jesus' healing; Nazareth a watch-tower; Hermon a sanctuary in the mountains; Moriah a mountain where Solomon built a temple; Ainon a place rich in water; and Jerusalem the centre of Palestine – a name modified in Wales to Salem or Caersalem. The use of such names in a country where there were hills, streams, lakes, mountain-top castles, heavy rain and lambs galore was intended to fortify in the congregations' minds the closeness of the association between their Wales and the land of the Scripture they studied.

CHAPTER 9

The Revivals

In Capel Hebron the choirs are singing,
And Martha and Jane and Hywel and Emrys
Are lost in the rapture of anthem and chorus
And the walls of the chapel are shaking with song,
And wave after wave of music crashes
Over the maddened multitude.
Chorus of Handel, mighty and glorious,
Rolls and reverberates again and again,
Tearing the barriers and bastions asunder,
Shaking the heart and the depths of the soul.
O spirit of music and wonder and passion
Flood with thy rapture our derelict valleys,
And give unto men the motion to action,
The impulse to build what is worthy of Man

Idris Davies, 'Capel Hebron', in A Book of Wales, *ed. D.M. Lloyd, Collins, 1961,*
courtesy of Faber & Faber

The revivals were an intrinsic part of the development of chapels from the early 1800s, and news of outbreaks spread quickly, sometimes resulting in smaller copy-cat revivals in other parts of Wales. The revivals had different characteristics: some were caused by a dramatic event like a spectacular conversion experience, the delivery of an especially potent sermon, the outcome of a turbulent prayer meeting, the inspirational effect of singing hymns, or the terror of an outbreak of the deadly cholera. The effect was extraordinary, and deeply personal, profoundly changing the individuals who were present, and it drove congregations to build chapels (121).

The pattern of Welsh revivalism began to emerge in the 1780s, and led to the most powerful and influential national revival in 1859. Much of the overpowering emotionalism of the revival syndrome appeared quite early in the evangelizing and preaching work of the Methodists. The characteristic wildness of congregations who were in an ecstatic trance was sneered at by the anti-Dissenters, and it should be noted that even the leaders of the Nonconformists themselves were wary of such unrestrained behaviour. The effect of the revivals was to change the social structure by creating, in the chapels, a highly-charged magnet, a force so powerful and overwhelming that it irresistibly drew in thousands of people to fill those chapels to overflowing, creating the need for more buildings.

The great national revival of 1858–59 was prefaced by a general slumber among the Nonconformists, and a lack of Enthusiasm. They carefully thought about how this religious torpor could be overcome, and how they might engineer a return to the heady days of contagious revivalism. News arrived in Wales of the outbreak of a vast revival in America in 1857–8, and the Welsh Nonconformist leaders were well aware of the 'implications and effects of such a divine visitation'. They were aided in their awareness of the impact of revivalism by their own memories of previous revivals in Wales; the publication in the 1850s of an examination of revivalism by John Hughes in his *Welsh Methodism*; the earlier presence in Wales of the American evangelist B.W. Chidlaw, of Ohio; the return to Wales of the Revd Humphrey Jones, who had seen American revivalism at first hand; the regular reports in *Drysorfa*; and the lecture delivered to Nonconformists gathered at Aberaman, Glam., in 1858, by D. Evans, and subsequently published as a book entitled *The Great Religious Awakening in America: God's Triumph over Mammon in the New World in 1858*, in which he compares the situation in Wales to pre-revival America (and suggests the obvious). Revival commentators often filled their journals with anecdotes and accounts of the characteristics of these often-mysterious manifestations, which give an insight into how affecting these events were. A partial list of revivals demonstrates both how numerous and how wide was the geographical spread, and gives a flavour of what they were like: 1762 Llangeitho;1778 Llanbryn-mair, Mont.; 1781 Llangeitho and Crug-y-bar, Carm.; 1782 Llanbryn-mair, Mont.; 1784 Tŵr-gwyn, Card.; 1785 Brynengan, Caern.; 1786 Trecastle; 1790 Llangeitho; 1791 Bala; 1805 Aberystwyth, Card. ('The Children's Revival'); 1811 Tŷ-mawr, Llŷn, Caern.; 1811 Llangeitho (the 'Quiet Revival'); 1817 Beddgelert; 1821 Bontuchel, Denbs.; 1822 Anglesey; 1828 Carmarthen; 1832 Caernarfon; 1833 Brynegan, Caern., and Llanystumdwy; 1837 Llanddeiniolen, Caern.; 1840 Merioneth; 1849 The South Wales Cholera Revival (there was another cholera revival in 1866 after an outbreak in Tredegar); 1850 Henllan; 1851 Staylittle, Mont.; 1855 Capel Isaac, Carm., and Trawsfynydd, Caern.; 1857 Trefeca, Brec.; 1858 Llanfairfechan; and in 1859 The Great National Revival, with outbreaks of revival fervour at Machynlleth, Aberdare, Llanfairfechan, Conwy, Aberystwyth, Pwllheli, Llangybi, Swansea, Aberafan, etc.

Observers of the two separate revivals described several phenomenal occurrences:

An unusual phenomenon of this revival was the 'singing in the air' which many reliable witnesses had heard. The sound of heavenly, angelic voices, sweetly and softly joined in harmony, without apparent melody, was overpowering. The effect on the hearers was to render them incapable of movement, as though nailed to the spot.

121 The great religious revivals crowded the chapels and made them inadequate, forcing the construction of thousands of new temples. Some revival meetings could not be contained by buildings, like the meeting at Bala depicted in this 1820 drawing.

During this revival prayer meetings were held underground at the lead-mines at Frongoch. One such meeting began at 6 a.m. upon the arrival of the early shift of miners, but it was said that 'Heaven penetrated in to the pit, and the Earth was forgotten.' When the afternoon shift descended they found the worshippers still at prayer in a sacred trance at 2 o'clock in the afternoon.

Some mines went as far as establishing a chapel within the pit itself – the 'seam-chapel' at Mynydd Newydd mine, Swansea, was 774 ft underground, another met in the weighing-house of a mine at Gaerwen, Ang. – and during these revivals the waiting-rooms of railway stations were pressed into service, as were malt-houses and various long-rooms at inns.

A prayer meeting was held at Blaenpennal chapel and though it was a tempestuous and stormy night, a multitude had attended. During the singing of the hymn 'He Who Speeds the Lightning's Flash' there was wild confusion. The chapel was overcome by Heavenly discords. The rejoicing and shouting was chaotic. Those who shouted were only rarely visible – they lay prostate in the dust, and only an arm occasionally thrown over the back of the seats would be seen. For ten months afterwards hardly a meeting would pass without an outburst of general jubilation.

This revival affected an enormous number of people, mostly Nonconformists, but new converts also flocked to the Anglican Church. Over 100,000 persons were converted during this revival (four-fifths of them were Nonconformists). It is not difficult to imagine the effect of such a national mass obsession with revival on the chapels. The size of the revivals and the pressures they put upon the chapels required a rapid reassessment of how they would fulfil their role. People flocked to the chapels in numbers never seen before: audiences previously attending theatres, taverns, drinking-clubs, and the music-halls abandoned these pursuits to be part of the revivalist congregation. Magistrates noted the sharp decline in public disorder and drunkenness, and even taverns closed for lack of trade. Rugby (the other 'national religion of Wales') was no match for the chapel, and some rugby clubs either cancelled fixtures or disbanded completely because the players had all been converted, were in the chapel instead of on the pitch, and their captain was now a preacher!

CHAPTER 10

Interiors: The Palaces of the Oral Arts

A n anonymous actor, visiting Wales, observed: 'Inside one is aware of the truly dramatic atmosphere of so many of the Welsh chapels, which, like the Elizabethan theatre style, have an intimacy which brings together actor and audience or pastor and flock, closely locked together in the business of drama or worship – or both.'

The Wesleyan Methodists called the period from 1850 to 1900 the Age of Mahogany, a reference to the increasingly lavish provision of interior finish in the new chapels. In truth, very little real mahogany made an appearance, but the finest pine and deal were cleverly comb-stained, varnished and lovingly polished to give the same effect. R.P. Jones, in his *Nonconformist Church Architecture* of 1914, was opposed to this and detested varnishes which 'cause high-lights: no material should have a greater polish than an egg-shell'. (He also noted that 'as to stained-glass, it may be said that like violin-playing, only the best is tolerable'!) Congregations in this age of 'mad facadism' were very competitive in the erection of a dramatic and attention-grabbing facade, but they equally insisted on finely-crafted and increasingly ornate interiors. The layout of the interiors, however, hardly ever varies, with the pulpit on the gable-end wall opposite the entrance doors, and, most often, a horseshoe-shaped gallery on three sides – in all this the Nonconformists readily conformed. The chapels of the last phase of chapel-building, up the outbreak of the First World War, become progressively encrusted with decorative elements and embellishments. While all the components to be found in the early chapels are still to be seen (for example, the pulpit and Big Seat arrangement), they are now loudly amplified and often expressed in a rather vulgar manner. These late interiors could not be further from the simplicity and austerity of the barn-chapels like Maesyronnen (Plates 1, 2) or Beiliheulog (Plates 4, 5), and the hands-on involvement of those early congregations was now replaced by, for example, the arrival in 1909 of Italian plasterers at Horeb, Penydarren, Merthyr (demolished), to install its beautiful ceiling, while the Ann Griffiths Chapel, Dolanog, Mont., Calvinistic Methodist, 1904, by W.G. Dickens-Lewis, dedicated to the memory of

122

Chapels were 'the Palaces of the Oral Arts' where the preachers were the masters of all they surveyed from their dominating pulpits. In modest chapels like Capel Mud, nr. Pen-y-sarn, Ang., 1777 and 1845 (122, Plate 22), there were simple and austere interiors; often in rural areas they could accommodate fewer than fifty people, as at Carmel Plas chapel, Llŷn, c. 1825 (123). Gedeon, Dinas Cross, Pemb., 1830, had two classes of seating – the bare benches in the gallery were for hardy non-members who did not have comfortable 'subscription pews' on the ground floor (124).

123

124

125 Some Baptist chapels had interior pools for baptism, but many rural folk suffered a frigid bath in an exposed outdoor pond, as here at Cwmsarn-ddu (under the corrugated iron covering in the foreground).

the hymnist, featured elaborate silk tapestry panels specified by the architect, with inspirational scenes from her life.

The interior of Capel Mud, Penygraig-wen, Ang., Baptist, 1777 and 1845 (abandoned) (122, Plate 22), serves as a good mid-nineteenth century rural example of a fully built-out interior, complete with oil-lamps, grandfather clock, deep box-pews on a sloping floor (no gallery), high pulpit, and small harmonium

126   **127**

The latter part of the nineteenth century was called the Age of Mahogany, with lavish interiors acting as huge display-cabinets of the carpenter's craft. The finest is the vast Tabernacl, Morriston, 1872 . . .

organ; also the tiny interior of Carmel, Carmel Plas, Llŷn, Caern., *c.* 1810 (123). The interior of Gedeon, Dinas Cross, Pemb., Congregational, 1830, is another – with a very simple set of bench forms in the gallery for non-members' use (124). (Some chapels, like Moriah, Pengenffordd, had exterior stairs that led to the gallery.) These interiors should be seen in comparison with the Greek 'cella' style interior of the Crane Street town chapel, Pontypool, 1847, with its very high quality of finish, substantial gallery and large organ – the pulpit is of exceptional interest as its front is a replay of the Greek facade of the building (back cover). The Baptists had a specific requirement of some chapel architects, to install a baptismal pool within the main body of the chapel, and in a place where the full-immersion ceremony could be witnessed. At Crane Street the pool is located under the floor of the large pulpit platform. Other chapels placed their pools on their plot of land, which meant a chillier open-air baptism, as at Cwnsarn-ddu, Llandovery, Carm. – in the graveyard opposite the chapel (125). The zenith of chapel interior-architecture is the mighty Tabernacl, Morriston, 1872, though the richly-decorated Plough chapel at Brecon, 1841 (128), is also in this category, as are the excellent pulpit and Big Seat at the Wesley chapel, Haverfordwest, 1866 (129), and George Morgan's Classic pulpit-apse at Newtown, 1881 (130).

The vast chapels of the late Victorian period employed all the new technologies

128   **129**

. . . but the 1841 interior of The Plough, Brecon (128), is also of exceptional quality. The
pulpit and the Big Seat of the Wesleyan chapel at Haverfordwest, 1866 (129), feature
elaborate carving, while George Morgan created an enormous marble-pillared apse at his
High Classic chapel for Newtown in 1881 (130).

130

available to the architect, with larger windows to light the chapels by day and 'gas-air' lighting for the evenings, and the congregation cosseted by the new low-pressure warming systems to cast the chill from their temple. Galleries in the last period of chapel-building become a standard feature, incorporated into the design from the outset. In many earlier chapels they were quite often inserted some years after the original building, to accommodate congregations swelled by revivalism. This was not always successful and some chapels had to plan on raising the roof in order to have enough headroom for those in the gallery, or dig out the floor. Some gallery insertions were subject to poor engineering and several collapsed. (At Cefn-mawr the entire Methodist chapel collapsed during a service, apparently through mining subsidence.) Most galleries were three-sided, U-shaped, though some completely circled the walls as a continuous ribbon, running above and behind the pulpit – which some observers found very distracting. The great Tabernacl, Morriston, is the best example of this trend as the gallery incorporates not only the organ, but tiers of stepped pews to accommodate great choirs. The galleries were supported by slim cast-iron columns made at the local foundries, with decorative bases and capitals. The frontage of the gallery was usually solid, but balustrades are common, as is a fine, light open metal screen in the form of stylized foliage – the Calvinistic Methodist chapel at Resolfen, Glam., 1904, by Beddoe Rees, £2,300, is an excellent town-chapel example (131), while Blaenannerch, Card., shows its use in a rural area (132).

The gallery was a vital contributor to the development of the congregational hymn-singing for which the Welsh gained world recognition, though by the end of the century one grumpy observer opined that 'The strains of solemn melody are often to be heard from within the chapel walls . . . but the compositions seem to be arranged that they serve the purpose of pleasing the singers more than producing devotion' (T.E. Clarke, 1850). The communal singing was, however, a great attraction for the younger members of the congregations and the introduction of the simple 'tonic *sol-fa*' system made it even more achievable. Tabernacle, Milford Haven, Pemb., Congregational, 1909, by D. Edward Thomas, was built with a choir gallery, arcaded side aisles, and wide curved seating, the whole interior having the feeling of a small Anglican church, rather than a Nonconformist chapel (133).

In every chapel, large or small, the focus is the pulpit – it is the one constant factor of Welsh Nonconformity that the people have gathered to see and hear the preacher, in an atmosphere of electric expectation, deliver *y Gair*, the Word of God, and to reflect on the meaning of *y bregeth*, the sermon. From the earliest chapel to the very last, the pulpit was raised to allow the congregation to hear and see the minister, but also to ensure that he could fix every member with his eagle eye and drive home the message to each and every person who sat before him. In some chapels the ground-floor pews were angled towards the pulpit in a 'spider-web'

131   132

Elegant counterpoints of colour, texture and materials are often found, with the solid flat
fronts of galleries sometimes replaced with light metal traceries in stylized plant forms, as at
the Methodist chapel by Beddoe Rees at Resolfen in 1904 (131). Blaenannerch's gallery
shows a similar airy treatment in the renovation of its chapel (132).

pattern, as at Bethel, Georgetown, Merthyr Tydfil, *c.* 1820, and the Baptist chapel,
1839, at Rhymni. The sermons, as we have seen, were far from abstract
interpretations of the Scriptures; they were forceful and eloquent discourses which
were intended to be readily understood by the listening congregation. The preachers
were well-informed about the events of the day, and used them to illuminate their
sermons – one minister said that the two best tools for a preacher were the Bible and
The Times! They were often very passionate – John Ruskin's view that good
preaching was 'half an hour to raise the dead' was the order of the day: the purpose
was to get the congregation to a door of understanding through the door of emotion.
The power of the preacher to rivet his listeners by unleashing a torrent of emphatic
rhythms and cadences in the sermons – called *hwyl* in Welsh – could sway
congregations into convulsive ecstasy.

The pulpit was always given special attention by the architect and the interior
carpenters and joiners, and they lavished their highest skills upon it, though the whole
interiors of these later chapels are literally showrooms of the carpenter's art. The early
pulpits were simple boxes, sometimes called 'preaching tubs', reached by a short stair,
but by the end of the nineteenth century many chapels redefined the pulpit and replaced
the box with a platform, which would be shared by a team of preachers, though this
style was also convenient for concert performances (Bethesda, Haverfordwest, Pemb.,

133 Galleries were an integral part of Welsh chapels, often being the location of the chapel choir, and thus made a vital contribution to the development of the national reputation for community choral singing that the Welsh enjoy. This gable-end gallery is at Tabernacl, Milford Haven, 1909.

Baptist, 1878). The preacher commanded the pulpit like a captain on the bridge of his ship, and some pulpits were popular for their excellent acoustics and view of the congregation, while others were feared. A notorious pulpit at Rehoboth, Hakin, Milford Haven, was a 'three-decker' of such height that some visiting ministers refused to ascend 'the perilous perch' and chose to speak from the safety of the Big Seat.

In the late chapels the pulpit and Big Seat complex was almost invariably placed on the gable-end wall opposite the entrance, which was very much in accord with the fondness of Victorian architects for 'architectural vistas'. It also emphasized the auditorium effect, though some critics felt that was a bad development. F.J. Jobson, in his *Chapel and School Architecture* of 1850, had already anticipated the problem, and spoke against the idea that a chapel was a warehouse for worship. Neither was it a concert hall or a theatre, it was the House of God. Jobson's comments were ignored by the later Victorian architects as they created even bigger concert-hall chapels, but others neatly identified why some Nonconformists were so unhappy with the sense of loss occasioned by this unstoppable architectural development:

134

In the late nineteenth century the little harmonium used to accompany choirs was replaced by huge powered organs. The cost was substantial – Priory Road Chapel in Milford Haven paid over £1,000 for its 1919 organ (134, also 100). Some congregations miscalculated the effect of inserting a large new organ, as at Llan-non in 1865 when it was installed against the facade wall and entirely blinded the two centre windows on the facade (135, also 60).

135

Formerly the preacher had stood up like the father of the family, with all the rest gathered around him, because the old style of building reflected Calvin's belief that the Communion was a supper round a table. Now the preacher is like a schoolmaster facing a class and the minister and the people are separated in a way against which the Puritans had protested.

Lismer Short, 'Evolution of Unitarian Church Buildings,' in H.J. McLachlan,
The Unitarian Heritage, *Sheffield, 1985*

Worse, the character of Christ had been the subject of a change of perception:

Christ was now seen as a popular minister, smiling but grave, enormously learned, wise and experienced, but full of help, understanding, generosity and fun. . . . Religion was seen to be a permanent Sunday School anniversary, Christ the affable lecturing minister, and the universe was a tidy chapel full of happy smiling faces.

The other and newer physical point of focus in these later chapel was the organ, which took on increasing significance. While a rural chapel like Capel Mud managed with a little harmonium, vast organ cases were installed in many chapels – adding considerably to the cost of the chapel. When Soar, Pen-y-graig, was built in 1832 the cost of the whole was £300, the new chapel in 1858 was £739, while the rebuild of 1903 was £5,705, of which £470 was for the organ alone. They were expensive investments, whereas a harmonium could be found for £19 (which is what Hermon, Nant-y-glo, paid the King Street Baptist chapel, Abertillery, for its used one in 1862). Seion, Llanelli, paid £471 for its organ in 1871 – a rural congregation might have built a whole new chapel for that sum in those days. The Priory Road Chapel, Milford Haven, paid over £1,000 for its new organ in 1919 (100, 134). The danger of the organ was that it was visually distracting and thus competition for the pulpit. Many architects specified that it should be located in the gallery opposite the pulpit, but there are many instances where the organ has been integrated into an architectural complex that fills the entire gable-end wall and unites the organ with the gallery, pulpit and Big Seat.

In his 1914 book *Nonconformist Church Architecture*, R.P. Jones offered advice about the problems of choirs and organs that many an earlier congregation could have heeded with valuable results:

In chapel design the first and most essential quality is REPOSE of effect; nothing should be tolerated . . . which is restless or distracting to the worshipper. . . . The custom of placing the organ directly behind and above the pulpit is entirely wrong. An organ, though capable of fine treatment, is far too complicated an object, decoratively, to form a good close to the vista and it distracts attention unwisely from the pulpit . . . while rows of variegated hats belonging to a mixed choir can produce a restless effect. . . .

In some chapels the organ was acquired years after the chapel was built, and there are many instances of it being rammed into a space that was never planned for it – at

136

Beddoe Rees's masterpiece, Ebenezer, Llandudno, 1909, a round interior under a large dome supported by slender pillars, with extraordinarily high standards of craftsmanship throughout the building. Ebenezer is a rare 'round chapel' . . .

137

138

139 . . . though there are some examples of half-round plans, like that of Tabernacl, Ruthin, 1889.

Llan-non, Card., the organ was installed in the 1865 chapel and completely obscured and blinded the two central facade windows (60, 135).

A very late-period interior possessed of remarkable qualities is Beddoe Rees's work at Ebenezer, Llandudno, Caern., Methodist, 1909 (136, 137, 138). He illustrated this chapel as a speculative building in his 1905 book *Chapel Building: Hints and Suggestions*, in which he also included a plan, to demonstrate that although the exterior shows a square building, the interior is a circular chapel beneath a large leaded cupola with a circlet of round windows, all supported on slender Classical columns. The quality of the interior finish is of the highest, notable especially in the woodworking skills required to execute the architect's design for piers of semi-circular pews, which are ringed by, literally, a circulating aisle. Ebenezer and the chapel at Groes (42) are the only round chapels left in Wales, though Tabernacl, Ruthin, Denbs., Presbyterian, 1889, by Thomas Williams (139), with a vast spray of organ-pipes, is an extended half-round and may be included in this category.

CHAPTER 11

The Late Nineteenth Century:
All Styles and No Styles

From the 1880s to the outbreak of the 1905 revival – which led to a final spurt of chapel-building – all the Nonconformist denominations saw a slow fall in membership. Without either a well-sustained membership, or a revival to swell a congregation, or passionate controversies that split a church and led to splinter-chapels being built, or any other stimulus – like cholera – there was far less need for new chapel buildings. (The unholy terror of cholera was a powerful congregation-builder – some 1,500 persons rushed to join the nine Independent chapels in Merthyr Tydfil during the 1849 outbreak.) The danger for the denominations was that the urgent drive for evangelism was long past and the late nineteenth-century Nonconformists had become comfortable, settled, part of established society, institutionalized and rather complacent – 'the flame that once ran though the stubble had dampened to a smouldering glow'. They remained essentially supine until roused from their nap by the 1905 revival when 'the mystic evangelist Evan Roberts came among the people as a prophet'.

Revivals had always spurred chapel-building, but the role of the chapel, especially in the revival periods, went far beyond being a place for worship. The great national revivals were notable for their encouragement of the building of not only bigger chapels, but secondary structures – the erection of an annexe, schoolroom, or the extension of the chapel vestry and its refurbishment. This was a return to the open-all-hours approach that had been a characteristic of chapels in the later 1700s, chapels that served the community in multiple ways. In large part this may have been in response to the repose of the Welsh Nonconformists, one of whom was to write, barely two years after the great 1905 revival, that Nonconformists were slipping back:

> On a cold, wet, stormy night, where will the people go, our young workers, where will they spend their time . . . if the chapel is shut? The chapel authorities do not dream of keeping the chapel open every evening, and especially Saturday evening, the evening of terrible temptations. . . . No, on Saturday the chapel must be kept clean for the following

140 A stone and coloured-brick extravaganza by R.G. Thomas at Castleton, 1858, with a wheel-window and dwarf tower, in a style that was sneered at as 'Bristol Byzantine'.

day. They think more about dust than souls, and more about the spider than they do about salvation. Our young people are falling away . . . the drinking-club with its expensive comfortable seating, its handsome furniture, its sparkling fire, its enticing music . . . is wide open, but the chapel is closed. Suitable buildings connected with the chapels should be provided for the young people. . . . Bible classes for both sexes, lantern lectures, places to sing and pray, and a good library provided.

Seren Gomer *denominational magazine, March 1907*

Slumbering though they may have been, even before the 1905 awakening revival the Nonconformists had built more chapels in Wales than in the whole of the rest of Britain, and more were yet to come: in 1910 a Royal Commission reported that there were 4,716 chapels standing in Wales, 800 of them in the industrial valleys of South Wales, 150 in the Rhondda Valley alone, where the 'trinity of chapel, works and rugby pitch' became a feature. The scale of chapel-building (and the provision of surplus accommodation, too) can be measured by one example: in 1905 the county of

 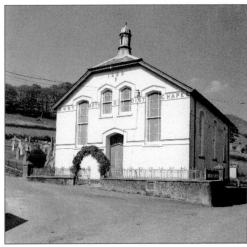

141   **142**

Late nineteenth-century reworking of facades often led to them being covered with a cement render to smooth over the evidence of the new works under a uniform finish. This allowed for dramatic colour schemes. Tabernacl, Cardigan, 1870 (141), and the unusual Cefn-Cwrt-y-Cadno of 1899, with its Meth-O-Dist denominational marker (142), show the trend.

Merioneth had 273 chapels and 34 churches, which could seat 75,800 persons. When those numbers are applied to the population of the county it meant that there were 307 places of worship for a total population of all ages and all faiths of 48,800 – one chapel or church for every 159 inhabitants.

Chapel-building in Wales ground to almost a complete halt in the decade leading up to the First World War, and after the slaughter had stopped and what was left of the troops had come home, it was found that they had no appetite for raising new Bethels. The great revival of 1905 had breathed new life into the Nonconformists and with renewed vigour they began to build new chapels in response to excited congregations and inflating membership. It did not last long. By the end of the previous century there had been a discernible change in the character of the Nonconformists, and of chapel membership: 'Nineteenth-century Nonconformity grew side-by-side with the growth of the middle class. The new and costly chapels reflected their pretensions . . . but by the end of the century those who had risen in the world tended to leave the chapel and return to the Church. The new generation of Welsh people who had breathed the atmosphere of the drawing-room, ball and social . . . found that the plain puritan worship of the chapels had no appeal' (T.M. Bassett, *The Welsh Baptists*, Ilston House Press, 1977). But while it did architects rose to the occasion and in a final flurry of chapel-building some of the most imposing as well as the most eccentric and awful temples were erected all over Wales. As

143

144

In spite of many truly meretricious buildings in the last years of the chapel-building era, a confident architect possessed of real skill could create a strong impact without resort to eccentricity – Richard Owen was able to do this for the Methodists with an imposing chapel at Llanidloes in 1874 (143), as was George Morgan in two very different chapels at Tabernacl, Merthyr Tydfil, 1898 (144), and his Mount Zion, Cardigan, twenty years before (145).

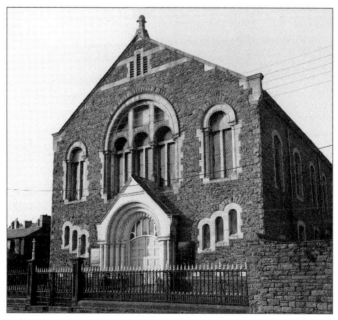

145

146

147
Laying the foundation stone and the opening of the chapel were great ceremonial occasions. A silver cement-trowel was often presented to the guest of honour who laid the stone – who was often a major donor to the chapel – as at Salem, Aberystwyth (146), while quite unique wooden tea-trays carved with a relief of the chapel, heralded by trumpeting angels, were given to guests of honour at Moriah, Llangefni, in 1897 (147).

The last revivals of the nineteenth century and the final call of the 1905 revival spurred a new chapel-building mania. Vast Nonconformist temples were erected, only to find a declining membership once the flush of revivalist enthusiasm had faded away. Jerusalem, Bethesda, 1890, is such a building (148), now demolished, that could find no young converts to carry its banner forward (149).

148

149

150

151

Architectural styles of all kinds appear, and the austerity of early chapels should be recalled in contrast to the huge spired town chapels like Seion (demolished) (150) and Salisbury Road chapels, Wrexham, 1878 (151), or the German church overtones of Siloam, Bontnewydd, 1896 (152).

152

153   **154**

Windsor Road Chapel, Caerphilly, 1903 (153), and Tabernacl, Milford Haven, 1909 (154), are in marked contrast to Libanus, Swansea (155) . . .

155

156   **157**

. . . or Bethesda, Tonpentre, 1909, and Moriah, Wattstown, Rhondda, 1909, but they all fulfil
the same basic function and have the same interior disposition as the very earliest chapels.

communication systems and transport had dramatically improved so had access to
information on what was going on in architecture, and historical texts became more
commonly available. They were contentedly looted by the chapel architects in their
search for new forms and devices, new novelties, and joined to themes which had
come from the most distinguished practitioners of the day. Every aspect of
architectural history was examined and exploited for motifs and forms that could be
incorporated into the new chapels.

The architects, as we have seen, were by no means bound by historical accuracy
when it came to creating a new chapel, and the collage approach was a guarantee of
idiosyncratic or eccentric designs, novelties, attention-grabbers, mournfully pompous
piles, stuffy Edwardianism, but also some wonderfully curious and charming
buildings. The Victorian architects were not at all interested in returning to a Welsh
past and reviving the puritanical austerity of the early chapel architecture, though
they would use every other style they could find. 'Hedonism' was not a word they
found embarrassing. Real innovation and originality became scarcer in the last period
of chapel-building, with the designers concentrating their efforts on manufactured
grandeur and engineering their facades for effect and impact.

Improved transportation allowed for the importation of materials not seen much before, with coloured slates, multi-hued Ruabon brick, terracotta panels, smooth cement blocks, elaborate dressed marble and exotic stone all being applied and accented. One of the most striking of these highly eclectic buildings is R.G. Thomas' Castleton, Mon., chapel for the Baptists in 1858, £2,000, in multi-coloured brick, with dwarf buttresses, a big wheel-window, tower and spire – a style that was mocked as 'Bristol Byzantine' (140).

Some architects chose to conceal the surface materials under a layer of cement, which they then painted over (Tabernacl, Cardigan, 1870 (141); Mount Pleasant, Holyhead, Ang., Independent, 1885, by Owen Morris Roberts (73); and Cwrt chapel, Cefn-Cwrt-y-Cadno, Card., 1899, with its inventive ribbon that divides the denominational identity into 'Meth O Dist') (142). Not all the buildings are the mannered mistakes of High Victorian eclectic architects, and though many lack merit, finely-scaled and strong facade treatments came from the hands of truly skilled and careful designers like Richard Owen (Wesleyan chapel and Calvinistic Methodist chapels at Llanidloes, Mont. (143), and Llandeilo, Carm., both 1874); the Revd William Jones (Bethel, Aberystwyth, Card., Baptist, 1888 (46), and the Calvinistic Methodist chapel, Llanidloes, Mont., 1902); Owen Morris Roberts (Moriah, Llangefni, Ang., Calvinistic Methodist, 1897, £5,500 (48)); the inventive George Morgan's Mount Zion, Cardigan, Baptist, 1878, for £1,200 (144), and his Tabernacl, Merthyr Tydfil, Glam., Baptist, 1898, £4,650 (145).

Congregations that had once been reticent in declaring their identity now did so with abandoned ardour, and an overweening pride in chapel-building became a characteristic of the late-period mania. Ceremonies attended by hundreds celebrated everything from the carrying of the first stone from the quarry, to the laying of the first dressed and inscribed foundation stone (often a row of them can be found on the lower facade, some even identify the architect: Beddoe Rees 'signed' his work at Resolfen with his name carved into a window sill). A symbolic mason's trowel, usually in silver, was sometimes presented to the chief guest, who was often the major contributor. The inevitable preaching and singing festival, with a tea-party, marked the opening of the new temple, and in the remarkable case of Moriah, Llangefni, in 1897, carved memorial tea-trays were given to the guests of honour, depicting the chapel, its opening heralded by trumpeter angels (147).

A glum institutional style developed that was rigidly sober, humourless, and more suited to civil purposes like banks, town halls, courts and jails, dour and often overscaled, their facades busy with encrusted architectural incidents or vast cave-like porches: Jerusalem, Bethesda, Caern., 1890 (demolished) (148). Huge town chapels with steeples, spirelets and towers appear: Seion, Wrexham, Denbs., 1878, by W. & G. Audsley, £5,500 (demolished) (150), had twin-spired towers, and Salisbury Road, also Wrexham, 1898 (151), are typical. Siloam, Bontnewydd, Caern., in 1896 has a dressed-stone surface that looks like a patchwork quilt, and also twin stepped towers and mini-cupolas of German inspiration (152). Peniel, Amlwch Port, Ang.,

158

159

The congregation of the Presbyterian chapel sent an architect to Italy in 1891 to copy a church there and erect its twin in Llandudno (158), a Ruthin congregation got a bow-front (159), another a terracotta facade (160), and Fishguard received the complex Beracah, 1906, marching up the hillside (161).

160

161

162   **163**

A knowledge of contemporary European architectural styles like Beaux Arts and Art
Nouveau appeared on some chapels – Beddoe Rees' Bethel at Llanwrtyd Wells, 1907, reveals
his wide-ranging interests (162); one of the very few post-First World War chapels, Bethel,
Cwmtwrch Isaf, 1925 (163), is a typical collage of disparate architectural elements.

Presbyterian, 1900, is an unusual throwback to the side-wall-facade tradition, but
with staircase bays and double porches stepping forward to greet the worshipper, all
with a strong Classical features (89).

Chapel architects in this period indulged themselves in the creation of buildings
that were occasionally exciting and dramatic, but most were idiosyncratic
concoctions, and the whole of the last twenty years of chapel-building is littered with
examples. Phillips & Wride designed the Windsor Road Chapel at Caerphilly, Glam.,
Calvinistic Methodist, 1903 (153), in a style that crosses a school with a factory, and
adds an impoverished campanile tower: the design is similar to the brick-and-
chequerboard facade of Tabernacle, Milford Haven, Pemb., Congregational, 1909, by
D. Edward Thomas (154). The 1905 Revival ensured the need for huge chapels, with
Libanus, Cwmbwrla, Swansea, Baptist, 1905 (155); Siloh, Llandudno, Caern., 1905,
by G.A. Humphries (117); Bethesda, Tonpentre, Glam., Independent, 1906, by W.D.
Morgan (156), and Moriah, Wattstown, Rhondda, 1909 (157), being good examples.
A member of the congregation of the Presbyterian church at Llandudno saw a fine
building while on holiday in Italy, and dispatched an architect from Wales to draw
and survey it – then had it built in Llandudno in 1891! (158)

164 'Grotesque but lovable . . . it stands like a toy castle in
front of a railway station.' Crwys Road Methodist chapel,
Cardiff, now serves a different denomination having been
converted to a mosque. When it was built by J.H. Phillips in
1899 he mixed Dutch gables, touches of the baroque, a whiff
of Classicism and a pinch of Art Nouveau, stirred well.
Nothing could be further from the 'honest-to-God' simplicity
of the grass-roots Welsh congregations who had built the
barn-chapels with their own hands and who had 'toiled
feverishly and persistently to make a dream into a temple'.

A bow-fronted chapel, Pen-dref, Congregational, had appeared in Ruthin, in 1875
(159), while a terracotta facade was applied at Moriah, Llanbedr, Mer., Calvinistic
Methodist, 1912 (160), and the late Classicism of the Revd William Jones travelled
from the Rhondda to the far west and created a powerful impression as Beracah, at
Fishguard, Calvinistic Methodist, 1906, for £1,700.

There are a few larger works by architects who were aware of the currency of the
Beaux Arts expression on the Continent, the Arts and Crafts and Art Nouveau in
Scotland and England, with Bethel, Llanwrtyd Wells, Brec., Calvinistic Methodist,
1907 (162), probably by Beddoe Rees, and his Bethania, Maesteg, Glam.; Bethel,
Cwm-twrch Isaf, Glam., in 1925, perhaps the very last gasp (163); and the remote
curious chapel near Llanarmon Dyffryn Ceiriog, Denbs., c. 1910 (Plate 20),
revealing this awareness.

Scattered among these are occasional eccentric works that provide cheery relief. The best of these are the Welsh Wesleyan chapel at Pontardawe, Glam., 1902, with a spray of wild typography on the upper facade; Beulah, Treorci, Glam., Baptist, 1909 (now an Apostolic church), with overtones of the French Beaux Arts school combined with a touch of British Nouveau; and the extraordinary Capel Crwys Road, Cardiff (now a mosque), by J.H. Phillips in 1899 (164), with references to Dutch baroque classicism and Art Nouveau. This last was memorably described as 'grotesque but lovable . . . it stands like a toy castle in front of a railway terminus . . . and was the end of the line for neo-Classical traditions in Welsh chapel architecture' (John Hilling, *Cardiff and the Valleys*, Lund Humphries, 1973).

The Welsh Nonconformists started in the eighteenth century by converting barns into chapels, built new ones, dressed them up, installed elaborate interiors, built bigger ones, and in the twentieth century have seen their temples empty and fading. Just after the outbreak of the last great revival, the Unitarians of Aberystwyth acquired the premises of a retiring bookseller (165). It had been built as a coach-house and horse-barn, converted into chapel. But it was too small for the congregation, who sold it, and it became an estate agent's offices, then the bookshop, until the Unitarians bought it, in 1906, put a new smart facade on to it, and converted this original barn back into a chapel. The wheel had come full circle.

165

CHAPTER 12

Befriending Friendless Chapels: Demolition and Documentation

In an explosive burst of building, the Nonconformist denominations in Wales erected over 5,000 chapels in the nineteenth century. Their enthusiasm was so great, and so contagious, that they were opening new chapels at a rate of more than one a week. Now they are closing at a rate of more than one a week, and the last two decades of the twentieth century have been desperate days for both the Nonconformists themselves, and for their chapel buildings. Distinguished buildings have been abandoned and demolished, while many have been converted for purposes as diverse as housing, furniture showrooms, a strip-club, garages, agricultural feed stores, factories, artists' studios, shops, bingo halls, squash courts, libraries, climbing centres, recording studios, a Women's Institute, a Masonic Hall, community centres, a boxing club, restaurants, an Institute for the Blind, a lingerie factory and the headquarters of the Welsh National Opera. Some of these conversions have been successful in retaining the essential architectural character of the chapel, but most conversions have paid little respect to such qualities or the distinctive presence the chapel has brought to its environment, and many examples of butchered Bethels are to be found all over the principality (Plates 21, 22, 23).

Not all chapel buildings can be saved, or indeed should be saved, but the best of them ought to be before the ravages of deferred maintenance, vandalism, the ministrations of the chapel-breaking salvage companies, weather, and sheer neglect render them unsavable. Little has been done in any coordinated way to record the chapels, even if we recognize the inevitability of massive loss of this architectural heritage, and only since about 1990 has there been a concerted effort to sensitize the nation to the immediacy of this potential loss. The excellent efforts of the volunteer group CAPEL, founded in 1986, the work of the Royal Commission on Historic Monuments in Wales, CADW, the Historic Buildings Council, the National Museums & Galleries and National Library of Wales, and the enthusiasm of dedicated friends

131

of friendless chapels are all beginning to have an impact. Even if we face the reality of the estimate that there will be over a thousand redundant chapels in Wales by the year 2005, and many will be demolished or drastically converted, the efforts of these bodies and individuals may as least preserve by documentation, photography, measured drawings, and securing the chapel records some large part of the fading chapel heritage.

A sensitized and interested public who are convinced that the chapel buildings may still have a role to play in their community is a vital need – if not as religious buildings, then playing an alternative role. The conversion of Glenala chapel in Llanelli to a community performance space is a simple example: it welcomes now not congregations but audiences to the restored building that retains its strong identity in the streetscape. Intelligent conversion of this kind can do wonders to preserve worthy buildings, but it requires an enlightened Council and planning officers to be steadfast in ensuring that every possibility of saving a building is explored before being so hasty as to permit a demolition.

In this book some of the extraordinary variety of expression in chapel architecture has been demonstrated, yet it hardly begins to reveal the richness of this heritage. In saving the best of Welsh chapels an assessment of the exterior quality is not the only criteria, as many chapels do not wear their hearts on their sleeves and do not reveal the quality of a magnificent interior behind a sometimes bland facade. We can be easily impressed by the robust and virile facade of the great chapels, and guess that the interior is its match, but what of the inconspicuous country chapels whose only feature is the simple but moving interior that speaks of the early days of Nonconformist faith in Wales. These modest preaching-rooms contain all the elements that we see in the great Victorian-Edwardian chapels, but compressed in an intimately-scaled and lamp-lit single-storey side-wall facade flat-floored box. Will we lose these treasures because their unprepossessing exteriors condemn them? We have already lost many of the chapels that were temples, community centres, libraries and schools. Identifying these best examples and affording them the protection of Listing is a matter of urgency. They are increasingly under threat. The decimation in the ranks of chapel buildings is accelerating – in the South Wales valleys they seem to be disappearing daily. Much has already been lost and without a coordinated national effort at preservation and documentation hundreds if not thousands of chapel buildings will vanish.

If only a handful are accorded protection as listed buildings, what of the rest? If they are to continue as places of devotion then the example set by some denominations in banding together the congregations from different deteriorating chapels in a district, and then meeting for worship in the best of their buildings, is one that others might follow. It is not easy for congregations to give up their traditional chapel home, but such a practical ecumenicism has a very positive impact on preserving the best examples. By pooling their efforts they can provide a worship-home for themselves, and protection for the building. Help should be provided to ensure the maintenance of such selected chapels – though the denominations themselves will not accept funds deriving from the National Lottery. Perhaps the Redundant Churches Fund of the Church of England may also provide a useful model, and that of the newer Historic Chapels Trust in England. The 1993 Welsh Affairs Committee Report *The Preservation of Historic Buildings and Ancient Monuments in Wales* recommended the creation of a fund specifically to aid in the preservation effort of chapels in Wales, and the Welsh Office has actively pursued setting up such a fund.

Conservation by documentation is vital. Only Mid Glamorgan and Clwyd authorities attempted a comprehensive survey of all the chapels in their counties, but a new national survey under the auspices of the Royal Commission, which began in 1995, will go far to ensure that a national record will be created. Nevertheless, consistent with the grass-roots origins of Nonconformity, the documentation and preservation of the material culture of the chapels in each county should be a high priority for the various local Councils. There is a step beyond this kind of conservation-by-documentation effort, which is the establishment of a national depository of material objects that relate to chapels – their records, ledgers, files, etc. – to ensure that this vital core of data is not lost. Given the huge number of chapels built in the second half of the nineteenth century, we should be seeing a constant stream of jubilee or centenary booklets about the chapels' history appearing – but the disadvantaged congregations nowadays cannot afford to produce them, and many chapels have already been abandoned and demolished without their history being written.

Some local authorities which receive applications for the demolition of chapels are becoming far more interested than heretofore in the preservation of chapels. They have been exercising their powers to protect and conserve a major existing example, but also to ensure that if conversion to a new purpose is proposed, that it be done with a sympathetic treatment that would retain the best qualities of the facade. This has not guaranteed the destructive alterations that have permanently disfigured many a Bethel, but it does show that there is a change of attitude and a great sensitivity. Given that the chapels of Wales have been dismissed *in toto* rather than selectively, and blanket criticism has promoted a prejudice that has allowed for wholesale demolition and carelessness, such a change in public perception is most welcome. In the past it has been a case of familiarity breeding contempt and ignorance tolerating neglect. There is, nevertheless, and in spite of the many losses, still time to make a cohesive effort to preserve the best of these virile expressions of Welsh building, but only if we continue to establish a coordinated and comprehensive effort to save the chapel heritage, the national architecture of Wales.

When account is taken of the average age of the membership of most Welsh chapel congregations, it seems as if the end of distinctively Welsh expressions of Christianity might be in sight, as those religious values dearest to earlier congregations are being more and more abandoned in a lingering but painfully inexorable process. The fire now burns on Cambria's altars only with a smoky and fitful flame, flickering hesitantly amid fast-cooling embers. . . . Nor is there any latter-day Elijah to be discerned on any mountain-top, charged with a prophetic charisma that once more might invoke the celestial lightning-flash. . . .

Glanmor Williams, The Welsh and their Religion, *University of Wales Press, 1991*

Appendix One

SPECIFICATIONS FOR A NEW CHAPEL, *c.* 1905

The architect Arthur O. Evans, of Pontypridd, drew up the plans for a new Baptist chapel, *c.* 1905, and wrote out the specification for the contractors. His preparation gives an insight into how a chapel architect would define his design for a new temple, carefully denoting everything from the kind of slate ('best North Wales slates from a quarry to be approved by the Architect') to the number of nails to be used to secure the floorboards ('two'), and the choice of a 'wrought iron gothic latch'. There follows a verbatim transcript of his handwritten instructions:

Specification of the several works to be done in the erecting of a Chapel at Hafod, Pontypridd, for the English Baptist Denomination, according to plans and specification prepared by Arthur O. Evans, Architect, Pontypridd.

The Contractor must visit the site and satisfy himself that all levels are correct.

The ground line in front elevation indicates the finished level of the centre of the road from which all levels must be taken.

At Completion the Contractor is to clean down all the premises and scrub the floors.

The Contractor is to provide in his estimate the sum of twenty pounds for contingencies to be spent as the Architect may direct which amount or any portion of it, if not spent is to be deducted from any monies due, or that may become due to the Contractor.

If called upon the Contractor must find two surities for the due and perfect completion of the work. The Contractor must sign the form of Contract provided by the Architect.

Excavation and Drains

The Contractor is to excavate for foundation for drain trenches, under wood floors for tank, to levels and widths shown and is to remove all earth from the site and deposit it on a site pointed out to him by the Architect. The Contractor is to well ram in the earth round the foundations and drain pipes when laid.

Drains: The Contractor is to open up Ground insert pinches in main drain and make good to the satisfaction of the surveyor of the Estate. Provide and lay 4 in and 6 in glazed earthenware drainpipes with socketted cemented joints where shown on block plan, the drains to be laid to regular fall and provided with all necessary bends and junctions.

Gullies: Provide & fix in Urinal a Ducketts gully with glazed earthenware dishing and 7 in hinged grating. Construct chamber where shown of 4 in brickwork with cement floor and cover with cast iron ventilator grating. Provide & fix in Urinal 4 in glazed gutter brick laid in cement.

Disconnector (NB): Provide & fix where directed a disconnector trap 30 shillings. No drains are to be covered over until they have been inspected and approved by the Architect.

Mason and Bricklayer

Stone: All stone to be native blue Pennant from a quarry approved by the Architect. All stone to be of regular colour and fixed on its natural face.

Bricks: All brick used in the dressings to be best pressed Cattybrook. All rough brick to be good hard well burnt brick.

Mortar: All mortar to be mill made, composed of one part Aberthaw brown lime to two parts of clean washed river sand or furnace ashes.

Concrete: All concrete to be composed of one part of Aberthaw lime, one of sand or Ashes, and three of broken stone to 3 in gauge.

Walling: All walling with the exception of the front to street to be good rubble walling well laid in mortar and packed in centre with at least two through stones to each yard super of walling. All exposed faces and both sides of boundary wall to be neatly pointed as the works proceeds.

Polled work: The whole of the front to be faced with paving. Cuttings in regular courses neatly bunker dressed square and true. the joints to be neatly rubbed with a jointer. no stone to be less than $1\frac{3}{4}$ in thick or more than $3\frac{1}{2}$ in. All paving cuttings must be from the same quarry.

Coping: The boundary wall coping is to be 18 in native stone set in mortar and roughly rounded. The boundary wall to be 6 ft 6 in high above ground and as shown on block plan.

Boundary wall: The front boundary wall to Chapel to be 3 ft 0 in high above ground and to be polled face on one side to be coped with 20 in × 24 in chisel dressed coping drilled for railings. Provide the sum of seventeen pounds for gates and railings.

Pillars: The four pillars to be 18 in square of best pressed brickwork, neatly pointed, fix on each a terra cotta cap, 15s 4*d*.

Angles: All angles to be true & plumb.

Jambs: All doors and windows to be revealed for frames, all window jambs to be splayed.

Brickwork: All brickwork in front to be tuck pointed, all other outside brickwork to be neatly flat pointed. The bricks to be cut and rubbed to door and window Arches. The moulded bricks in window labels to be neatly cut rubbed and mitred at inter-sections, moulded terra cotta stops to be provided to label courses. The upper courses of bricks in plinth to be champfered. Bricks in arches to be cut & rubbed, properly radialed & neatly pointed. The cornice caps & pediment to be formed by projecting courses of square brick. The upper course in each case to be laid in cement. All quoins except front to project $\frac{3}{4}$ in from face of work.

Chimneys: The chimneys to be best pressed Cattybrook flat pointed with plain oversailing courses all laid in cement and to have fixed on top two red dwarf Chimney pots.

WC & Urinal: To be built of $4\frac{1}{2}$ in B.P. Brickwork Cattybrook neatly laid flat pointed the four upper courses of urinal to be laid in cement.

Mullions: The brick mullions in windows to be carefully tied in every course, & carefully built.

Arches: Brick relieving arches are to be turned over all openings. The 9 in brick wall to be very carefully and truly built, the exposed portion above vestry roofs to be prepared for cementing.

Fireplaces: Build fireplaces where shown with 9 in brick Arches over each 3 ft 0 in from floors level. 2 in Chisel dressed hearth stones, and construct 9 in × 9 in flue properly pargetted, provide the sum of £2 10*d* 0*s* for two grates & mantles which the contractor must fix finding all materials.

Ventilators: Provide & fix in walls eight 9 in × 9 in wrought iron gratings and form 9 in × 9 in Channels to ventilate under floors. Construct eight 12 in × 12 in Channels through walls & 9 in × 12 in vertical ventflues on them to 6 ft 0 in above floor. Provide & fit 12 in × 12 in wrought iron gratings outside and inlet hoppers 7*s* 6*d* inside.

Paving, Steps & Sills

Paving: Pave the Urinal, WC and form front gate to entrance steps, with 2 in paving dressed 1 in in and laid in mortar on 4 in of hard dry material that in Urinal to be laid to fall to gutter.

Steps: The front entrance steps to be 16 in × 7 in Chisel dressed all other door steps to be 12 in × 4 in dressed on edge.

Sills: All sills to be of Forest stone weathered with stoalings left on & Chisel dressed 10 in × 11 in.

Damp Course: Lay under whole surface of walls below wall plate, damp Course ¾ in thick of sand pitch and tar.

Tiles: Provide & fit in lobby on 6 in of Concrete tiles 4*s* 3*d* per yard super, tile to be truly laid in cement.

Slate Slabs: Provide & fit against walls & for divisions planed slate slabs 1¾ in thick with rounded edges and securely fixed to wall by iron clamps & pointed with cement.

Carpenter & Joiner

All timber to be sound and free from sap, large loose or dead knots or shakes, and to hold the size specified when fixed, no joists or rafter to be fixed more than 15 in centre to centre. All wall plates to be bedded in mortar.

All joiners work to be best quality Red Baltic.

All Carpenters work to be of best white deal.

The exposed roof timbers to be of best red as above or best Pitch Pine and wrought. Provide and fix over all openings lintels 1 in thick for every foot of opening but in no case less than 3 in.

Roof: This roof to be formed with three frame collar bearing King post principals formed with 11 in × 4 in blades & collar 9 in × 3 in King post and 4½ in × 3 in strutts framed & bolted together & provided with 2 in × ½ in wrought iron straps and ⅝ in bolts as shown in sketches.

The principals to rest on template 1 ft 6 in × 11 in × 3 in fix to each shaped curbed rebs 3 in thick with 3½ in mould mitred all round, the exposed part of principals to be wrought & stop chamfered. Purlins 5 in × 7 in wall plates and 4 in × 3 in ridge 9 in × 1½ in Common rafters & ceiling joists 3 in × 2 in projecting 9 in over wall. barge boards 11 in × 2 in stop Ch'd with 3 in band mould under slates & wrought shaped end.

Vestry roof: To have three half principals with blades 9 in, part wrought and chamf'd, purlins 5½ in × 4½ in common rafters, ceiling joists and wall plates 3 in × 2 in, faced 7 in × 1 in beaded, barge boards 9 in × 1½ in chamfered with shaped ends & 2½ in band mould under plates. WC Common rafters ceiling joists & wall plates 3 in × 2 in eaves 7 in × 1 in beaded barge boards 7 in × 1½ in Chamf'd. Trim rafters to chimney. Trim rafters over vestry and in two places in school for manhole 2 ft 0 in × 2 ft 0 in case with 4 in rebated & beaded casing with 2½ in band mould all round and fit into manhole ¾ in boarding cut fretwork to detail to be supplied.

Ventilators: Provide over chapel manholes two zinc tubes tapering to 12 in to fit into 12 in roof ventilator £3 0*d* 0*s* each which the contractor is to provide & fix over the manholes, provide & fix in tube adix valve on pivots with seating, & cords pullies & cleats to open & shut same.

Wallplates: Fix along junction of wall & ceiling in schoolroom 4 in × 4½ in in moulded plate.

Floors: All wallplates to be 3 in × 2 in, joints 7 in × 12 in & lay on best spruce flooring 7 in × 1 in closly laid, nailed with two nails to each joist with splayed headings, no two joints to come together to be mitred to hearth. The floor of the Deacons pew to be 15 in above rest of floor with two steps 7 risers formed each side.

Doors and Entrance: Provide & fix 5½ in × 4 in rebated & beaded frame heads transome & hang in same with two pairs 5 in butts 2½ in framed panelled moulded folding doors & provide with wrought iron gothic latch, strong 9 in oak cased lock, monkey tail bolt & 12 in barrel bolt.

The two openings to lobby & four doors to vestry to have 4½ in × 3½ in rebated & stop chamfered frames & heads & hang in these six openings with 3 in butts, 2 in framed six panelled double moulded doors each have a strong 6 in mortice lock and heavy brass furniture. the two external doors to lobbies to have two 9 in barrel bolts each. The WC urinal & boundary wall door openings to have 4 in × 3 in rebated & beaded frames & hang in same with 3 in butts 1½ in framed ledged beaded doors with strong brass furniture. The two external doors to lobbies to have transomes & 2 in rebated and moulded fixed sashes 1–6 in high. Provide & fix round all doors where frame or casing is flush with plaster. 4 in moulded architrave finishing on 4 in blocks.

Windows: Provide & fix to all window openings 4 in × 3 in rebated & headed frames, 4 in × 2 in mullions and transoms. Circular framed heads & 4 in × 3½ in sunk and weathered & fix in same 1½ in rebated moulded sashes with glazing bars as shown 1 in round nosed window boards with return ends & 1 in scotia under to be fixed to all windows, these to be fixed level. Provide for hanging two panels or panes in each window with 3 in butts & provide & fix opener with cords 6s 6d each.

Chair rail – dado: Provide & fix round rooms where shown 4 in × 2½ in. Chair rail securely plugged to wall as a capping and ¾ in V-jointed 4 in matchboard dado round chapel vestries & lobby.

Skirting: Provide & Securely plug to all walls 12 in chamfered skirting mitred to all angles WC skirting board to be 7 in.

Quoin beads: Provide to all internal angles to which plaster is to be quirked.

Pulpit: Provide the sum of £28 for pulpit & Deacons pew to be carried out to detail.

Tank: The tank to be built of 9 in brickwork laid in white Hygenic cement on 6 in of concrete.

Provide & fix in floor a 5 in × 4 in rebated framed ledged cover in three pieces with rebated points each piece to have two sunk iron rings.

A moveable flight of steps to be provided from floor level to bottom of tank with 3½ in × 3½ in square chamfered newel 10 in × 1½ in strings and 8 in × 2 in treads housed into the strings.

Plumber and Ironfounder

Eaves: Provide to all eaves 4 in half round cast-iron gutter with cast iron stop ends outlets and angles, to be well secured to common rafters by strong wrought iron straps two to each length & secured with red lead, nuts & bolts.

Downpipes: Provide & fix the following stack of 3 in round cast iron down pipe securely fixed by two wrought iron hoops to each lengths, & provided with cast iron heads, shoes and plinth bends. Two stacks each side of main roof and one from WC.

Lead: All lead used to be 6lbs to the foot super, no solder joints will be allowed.

Wherever slates abut against walling or brickwork zinc soakers turned up 2 in against wall & lead flashings built into wall 2 in turned down 4 in (and on slates where it is an apron 6 in) are to be provided, flashings to be pointed with cement.

Water: Arrange with Water Coy. pay all fees & lay on ¾ in heavy lead service pipe with ½ in branches to Baptistry.

WC tank, Urinal, and to corner of vestry with a ½ in brass screw down draw off cock is to be provided.

Tank: Provide & fix in floor 3 in brass seating & plug with chain securely bedded in the brickwork.

Stop Cock: Provide & fix under street paving a full way brass stop cock & provide & fix cast iron cover box to same.

WC: Provide & fix a wash down combination pan seat cast iron seat brackets 2 Gallon flushing tank 1¼ in lead flashing pipe chain & pull to satisfaction of Architect.

Ventpipe: provide & fix 4: Cast iron vent pipe jointed with lead carried 3 ft 0 in above eaves & to have patent exhaust cowl.

Gas: Pay Gas Coy. for laying in service, provide & fix through building compo. service piping where directed & provide & fix fixtures for service & fixtures, the sum of ten pounds is to be provided.

Slater

Cover all roofs with best North Wales slate 24 in × 12 in from a quarry to be approved by the Architect, to be nailed with 2 in compo nails, two to each slate to 3½ in lap to 2 in × 1 in battens to be double to all eaves & carefully cut to valleys.

Ridge: Provide & fix on crest plain red tile terra cotta ridge tiles set in cement.

Plasterer

Putty to be of white lime run at least 5 weeks before being used, a proper proportion of hair to be mixed with the mortar. All walls unless otherwise described to be rendered floated & then set with lime stucco of Nantes sand to perfectly true surface. All ceilings to be lathed and plastered two coats. Walls of WC to be plastered two coats.

Cement two coats, one Portland cement to 3 of Nantes sand, exposed portion of 9 in brick wall in back.

Painter & Glazier; Stain & Varnish: The exposed roof timbers, moulded wall plates window boards, manholes & chair rail & dado to be sized, stained & varnished two coats with best Copal Varnish.

Paint: All other woodwork usually painted to be knotted & primed and then receive three coats oil paint the finishing tint to be selected by the Architect. All outside wood to be varnished.

Glazing: All windows & fanlights to be glazed with Harkleys ⅛ in rolled glass, well puttied.

Arthur O. Evans, Architect

Appendix Two

THE ACCOUNT OF BUILDING CAPEL NEWYDD, LAMPETER, 1904

Although many congregations were mired in a debt for chapel-building that would not be cleared for decades, a good number were able actually to raise the money as the contractor erected the chapel by borrowing on the basis of promised gifts, a collateral of subscriptions. Most chapel histories reveal the bottom-line cost of the building, but this particularly specific account gives in full exactly how the work was executed and the costs apportioned:

Capel Newydd 'Brondeifi', Lampeter, 1904

Expenditure:

Cheque book	£0 3s 0d
Architect's fees	£74 0s 0d
Contractor, for taking down the old chapel and building new	£1,899 0s 3d
T. Davies, Lampeter, for gate	£7 11s 5d
W. Williams, Postgwyn, for work done on gate pillars and outside building	£3 2s 0d
D. Davies, Landdewi, for gate pillars	£0 12s 0d
A. Price, Lampeter, painting schoolroom	£7 0s 0d
T. Roberts, Lampeter, plumber	£23 10s 0d
Advertisements	£4 10s 0d
T. Richards, Ardwyn	£1 0s 9d
J. Hughes Evans, Lampeter, linoleum	£1 19s 2d
Jones, Lampeter, carpenter, materials for outside building	£1 16s 4d
J.E. Lloyd, Lampeter, Solicitor	£1 1s 1d
D. Evans, Cilgellisaf, Lampeter, interest on money borrowed	£5 0s 0d
L & P Bank Interest	£6 13s 9d
D.R. Evans & Co., Lampeter	£3 5s 0d
Postage and the Statement of Accounts	£0 19s 6d
TOTAL:	£2,043 3s 7d

Against this total expenditure they raised subscriptions from persons they could name to the amount of £2,040 0s 3d, a further 6s 3d from persons whose names they had lost, and incurred bank interest of £2 17s 1d. That all came to £2,043 3s 7d, which is what Capel Newydd had cost them, and it opened in 1904 with its debt cleared.

Bibliography

T.M. Bassett, *The Welsh Baptists*, Swansea, Ilston House Press, 1977

Peter Benes, *New England Meetinghouse and Church*: 1630–1850, Boston University Press, 1979

John Betjeman, *First and Last Loves*, John Murray, 1969

Clyde Binfield, *So Down to Prayers*, Dent, 1977

Marcus Binney, *Churches and Chapels: Who Cares?*, British Tourist Authority, 1977

Martin Briggs, *Puritan Architecture and its Future*, London, 1946

George Dolby, *The Architectural Expression of Methodism*, Epworth Press, 1964

E.D. Evans, *A History of Wales 1660–1815*, and D. Gareth Evans, *A History of Wales 1815–1906*, Cardiff, University of Wales Press, 1989

Ralph Griffiths (Ed.), *The City of Swansea*, Alan Sutton Publishing, 1991

John Harvey, *The Art of Piety*, Cardiff, University of Wales Press, 1995

John Hilling, *Cardiff and the Valleys*, Lund Humphries, 1973

John Hilling, *The Historic Architecture of Wales*, Cardiff, University of Wales Press, 1979

J. Geraint Jenkins, *Life and Traditions in Rural Wales*, Dent, 1976

Anthony Jones, *Chapel Architecture in Merthyr Tydfil*, Merthyr Libraries, 1962

Anthony Jones, *Welsh Chapels*, National Museum of Wales, 1984

Ieuan Gwynedd Jones, *The 1851 Religious Census: The Returns for Wales* (two volumes), Cardiff, University of Wales Press

BIBLIOGRAPHY

J.R. Jones, *The Welsh Builder on Merseyside*, Liverpool, 1946

Penri Jones, *Capeli Cymru*, Y Lolfa Press, 1980

R.P. Jones, *Nonconformist Church Architecture*, The Lindsey Press, 1914

Kenneth Lindley, *Chapels and Meetinghouses*, John Baker, 1969

Michael Llewellyn, *The Sand in the Glass*, John Murray, 1943

H.J. McLachlan, *The Unitarian Heritage*, Sheffield, 1985

The Perfidious Welshman and The Welshman's Reputation, by anonymous authors, Stanley Paul, 1910

Iorweth Peate, *The Welsh House*, Liverpool, Brython Press, 1946

Perkins & Hearne, *The Methodist Church Builds Again*, Epworth Press, 1946

D. Ben Rees, *Chapels in the Valley*, Ffynnon Press, 1975

Thomas Rees, *History of Protestant Nonconformity in Wales*, John Snow, 1883

Peter Smith, *Houses of the Welsh Countryside*, HMSO, 1975

David Walker, *History of the Church in Wales*, Church in Wales Press, 1976

Welsh Arts Council, *Recording Wales 2: Chapels*, 1969

James F. White, *Protestant Worship and Church Architecture*, Oxford University Press, 1964

Eurwyn Wiliam, *Home-made Homes*, National Museum of Wales, 1988

Glanmor Williams, *The Welsh and their Religion*, University of Wales Press, 1991

Gwyn Williams, *When was Wales?*, Penguin, 1985

Index of People and Places

Page numbers in italics denote black and white illustrations; page numbers in bold denote colour illustrations.